COLLOQUIAL

Persian

THE COLLOQUIAL SERIES

---

*Colloquial Arabic of Egypt
*Colloquial Arabic (Levantine)
*Colloquial Arabic of the Gulf and Saudi Arabia
*Colloquial Chinese
*Colloquial Czech
 Colloquial Dutch
*Colloquial English
 Colloquial French
 Colloquial German
 Colloquial Greek
*Colloquial Hungarian
 Colloquial Italian
 Colloquial Japanese
*Colloquial Persian
*Colloquial Polish
 Colloquial Portuguese
 Colloquial Romanian
 Colloquial Russian
*Colloquial Serbo-Croat
 Colloquial Spanish
 Colloquial Turkish

*Accompanying cassette available

COLLOQUIAL
Persian

Leila Moshiri

ROUTLEDGE
LONDON AND NEW YORK

For my parents

First published in 1988 by
Routledge
11 New Fetter Lane, London EC4P 4EE
29 West 35th Street, New York, NY 10001

© *Leila Moshiri 1988*

Set in Linotron Times
by Input Typesetting Ltd, London
and printed in Great Britain
by Cox & Wyman Ltd
Reading, Berks

British Library Cataloguing in Publication Data available

Library of Congress Cataloging in Publication Data
Moshiri, Leila, 1943–
    Colloquial Persian.
    (The Colloquial series)
    "Published in the USA . . . in association with
    Routledge, Chapman and Hall, Inc."—T.p. verso.
    1. Persian language—Spoken Persian.   2. Persian
language—Grammar—1950–   .   I. Title.
PK6224.8.M67   1988   491'.5582421   87–28500

ISBN 0–415–00886–7
ISBN 0–415–00887–5 (cassette)
ISBN 0–415–2618–0 (book and cassette course)

Contents

Introduction   1

Abbreviations   3

The Persian Alphabet   4

Pronunciation   6
Stress and Intonation; Consonants; Vowels; Diphthongs; Alteration of Vowel Sounds in Colloquial Speech; Capital Letters and Punctuation

Lesson 1   11
Articles; Gender; **-e/ast**, **hast**, **nist**; Word Order; Plurals; Interrogatives; And; Phrases and Expressions

Lesson 2   19
Subject Pronouns; The *ezāfe*; Adjectives; Comparison of Adjectives; Demonstratives; Phrases and Expressions

Lesson 3   28
Verbs I: the infinitive; tenses formed from the past stem – simple past, imperfect and past participle; The Verb 'to be'; Phrases and Expressions

Lesson 4   38
Verbs II: tenses formed from the present stem – present tense, subjunctive, imperative, Noun of the Agent; Phrases and Expressions

Lesson 5   49
Use of the Particle **rā**; Compound Verbs; Compound Tenses – perfect, pluperfect, future, past subjunctive, passive; Phrases and Expressions; Summary of Verb Endings

Lesson 6   61
Adverbs and Adverbial Expressions; Prepositions; Phrases and
Expressions

Lesson 7   71
Numbers; Phrases and Expressions

Lesson 8   79
The Calendar; The Seasons; The Days of the Week; The Points
of the Compass; Telling the Time; Currency; Expressions of
Time

Lesson 9   87
Pronouns – possessive pronouns, interrogative pronouns, indefi-
nite pronouns, **khod**, colloquial use of pronominal suffixes;
Colloquial Use of the *ezāfe*; Conjunctions; Phrases and
Expressions

Lesson 10   96
Subordinate Clauses – relative clauses, indirect statements,
wishes and commands, result clauses, conditional sentences,
possibility; Impersonal Constructions; Phrases and Expressions

Lesson 11   105
Word Formation

Lesson 12   110
Polite Phrases and Conventions; Other Expressions

Situational Phrases and Conversations: 113
At the Airport; At the Travel Agent; Shopping; Asking the Way;
The Telephone

Appendix   120
Numbers; Currency; The Calendar

Exercise key   123

English-Persian glossary   129

Persian-English glossary   185

Introduction

The country is Iran, its people are Iranians, but things and the language are Persian. The Iranians themselves refer to their language as **fārsi** because whereas the country as a whole derived its name from the Aryan peoples who first migrated there, the predominant tongue came to be that of the people of Fars, the province which held Persepolis, the capital of the Persian empire of two thousand years ago.

Persian is an Indo-European language, which means that it is related to the languages of Western Europe (when you come to them, you may like to compare the words for father, mother, daughter, brother, with English or German). After the Islamic conquest of Iran, Arabic became for a time the language of officialdom and learning with the result that Persian itself came to be written with the Arabic alphabet and there was an enormous Arabic influence on the language in terms of vocabulary, though hardly any in terms of its basic structure which retained its own identity. There is usually a pure Persian equivalent for most Arabic borrowings, but one or the other has tended to become dominant and more normally used. This is rather like the French borrowings in English after the Norman conquest. In the 1960s and 1970s a conscious effort was made to reduce the use of Arabic words, but with the return to an Islamic society and the greater emphasis that is now placed on the teaching of Arabic and the learning of the Koran in schools, this trend has been reversed. It is probably worth noting, however, that many words of Arabic origin used in modern Persian have acquired a different meaning or shade of meaning from that of present-day Arabic.

Colloquial Persian is the language of ordinary speech and conversation. It is not written down, except nowadays in informal correspondence between young people. The main difference between the spoken word and the written language is in the alteration of vowel sounds, the contractions that occur in many forms of the verbs and the colloquial use of the many suffixes. It is quite difficult to draw a definite line between the conversational language and more formal speech, not because the two forms are interchangeable, but because both forms will be heard, depending on the circumstances in which you may find yourself. Native speakers always address each other in colloquial Persian, but since they do not write as they speak, anything being read, such as the radio or television news, official reports, etc, will be in the correct forms which would sound stilted if used in conversation. It is partly for this reason that the language cannot be learnt properly without some basic knowledge of the correct forms which are then altered in speech. I have tried, however, not to err too much in this direction.

It may be of interest to note that a number of other languages are spoken in the different regions of Iran, chief among which are Turkish in the north-western province of Azarbaijan and an Arabic dialect in the South. There are also Kurdish and Baluchi, and the dialect of the Caspian province of Gilan. There is a sizeable Armenian minority in the country, chiefly in Tehran and Isphahan. People who are native speakers of any of these languages will tend to have varying degrees of accent when speaking Persian and this has little to do with the degree of education of the speaker. The standard pronunciation is that of Tehran which is used in this book.

A cassette has been produced to accompany this book so that you can hear Persian spoken by native speakers. All material on the cassette is marked by a ■ in the text.

Abbreviations

The following abbreviations have been used in this book:

adj.	adjective
adv.	adverb
anat.	anatomical
coll.	colloquial
conj.	conjunction
etc.	etcetera
excl.	exclamation
fig.	figurative
geog.	geographical
govt	government
interrog.	interrogative
intrans.	intransitive
lit.	literally
mech.	mechanical
mil.	military
n.	noun
pl.	plural
prep.	preposition
s.o.	someone
sing.	singular
sth.	something
trans.	transitive
usu.	usually
vb.	verb

The Persian Alphabet

As a matter of interest, the Persian alphabet is set out below, together with the transcription used in this book. It is important to realise that the letters change their shape according to the position they occupy in the word, and for the sake of simplicity only the initial forms and the final, unjoined forms of the letters are shown here.

Name	Final, unjoined form	Initial form	Transcription
alef	ا	ا آ	ā, a, e, o, u
be	ب	ب	b
pe	پ	پ	p
te	ت	ت	t
se	ث	ث	s
jim	ج	ج	j
che	چ	چ	ch
he	ح	ح	h
khe	خ	خ	kh
dāl	د	د	d
zāl	ذ	ذ	z
re	ر	ر	r
ze	ز	ز	z
zhe	ژ	ژ	zh
sin	س	س	s
shin	ش	ش	sh
sād	ص	ص	s
zād	ض	ض	z

tā	ط	ط	t
zā	ظ	ظ	z
êin	ع	ء	'
ghêin	غ	غ	gh
fe	ف	ف	f
ghāf	ق	ق	gh
kāf	ک	ک	k
gāf	گ	گ	g
lām	ل	ل	l
mim	م	م	m
nun	ن	ن	n
vāv	و	و	v, ow
he	ه	ه	h
ye	ی	ی	y, i, êi

Pronunciation

It is very difficult to render the pronunciation in transliteration of any language not written with the Roman alphabet. I have tried to keep the following guide as simple and accurate as possible, but correct pronunciation can really only be achieved by hearing and imitating native speech and for this purpose the accompanying cassette will be found to be extremely valuable, if not essential.

STRESS AND INTONATION

As a general rule the stress in Persian falls on the last syllable of the word. The main exceptions to this are in words with the various verb endings and some suffixes, which will be indicated as they occur, and words with the negative prefixes. Persian makes intensive use of prefixes and suffixes, but in general words tend to retain their basic stress pattern even when the number of syllables is altered by such additions:

e.g. **ketàb – ketàbi – ketàbam – ketàbe sefid.**

Intonation is also used a great deal to give variety of expression, but apart from mentioning the interrogative tone used for questions, the rest can really only be learnt by ear.

■ 1. CONSONANTS

(*a*) Pronounced as in English:

b	m
d	n
f	p
g – hard as in *get*	s – as in *sit*
h	t
j	v
k	y
l	z

(*b*) **r** – trilled, try saying *brrrr*
    kh – as in the Scots *loch*
    sh – as in *sheep*
    ch – as in *chat, chap*
    zh – like the j in the French *je*
    gh – there is no corresponding English sound; pronunciation of this letter should be learnt from native speakers. You can achieve an approximation by sticking the very back of your tongue to the roof of your mouth and then letting go, letting breath and sound out at the same time.

Where any of the above letters appear without the joining line underneath, each will have its own value as a consonant.

(*c*) **'** – the glottal stop:

The closest to this in English is in the cockney *bo'le*, for 'bottle'. This sound is not as strong in Persian as it is in Arabic. Between two vowels **'** really only separates them:
sā'at (watch, time), **etā'at** (obedience)

It is slightly stronger between a vowel and a consonant:
ta'mir (repair), **fe'lan** (for the time being)
likewise after a consonant at the end of a word:
rob' (quarter)

(*d*) Double consonants (called **tashdid** in Persian):

The sound of the consonant is reinforced, so that each consonant is almost pronounced separately, rather like the English word boo*k-c*ase:
najjār (carpenter)
It is rather like coming down on the first letter then taking off again from the second.

■ 2. VOWELS

ā – as in *wash*, or the *o* in *on*	**bābā** (daddy)
a – as in *hat*	**bad** (bad)
e – as in *end*	**khāne** (house), **esm** (name)
i – as in *deed*	**in** (this)

o – as in the French *mot*   **bozorg** (big), **do<u>kh</u>tar** (girl)
u – as in *ooh*   **hulu** (peach)

■ 3. DIPHTHONGS

êı – as in *raid*   **êınak** (spectacles)
ow – as in *mow*   **mowz** (banana)

Where two vowels appear together in the text with no connecting line on top, each vowel will have its own value and must be pronounced separately.

■ Pronunciation Exercises

ā   **ālu** (plum); **āb** (water); **ārd** (flour); **bālā** (up); **bād** (wind)

a   **ast** (is); **abru** (eyebrow); **namak** (salt); **bad** (bad)

e   **esm** (name); **emārat** (building); **nefrat** (hate); **negāh** (look); **<u>kh</u>āne** (house); **rānande** (driver); **entezār** (waiting)

i   **in** (this); **injā** (here); **imān** (faith); **bebin** (look!); **bidār** (awake); **bimār** (ill); **ābi** (blue); **zendegi** (life)

o   **oftād** (he fell); **otā<u>gh</u>** (room); **bozorg** (big); **do<u>kh</u>tar** (girl)

u   **un** (that); **hulu** (peach); **utu** (iron); **ārezu** (wish)

êı   **êınak** (spectacles); **êıvān** (verandah, balcony); **mêıdān** (square); **bêıne** (between)

■ 4. ALTERATION OF VOWEL SOUNDS IN COLLOQUIAL SPEECH

(a) The vowel **ā** almost always becomes **u** before an **n** and frequently also before an **m**:
<u>kh</u>āne (house) becomes **<u>kh</u>une**, **nān** (bread) becomes **nun**, **āmad** (he came) can become **umad**.

(b) Vowels followed by two consonants at the end of a word are lengthened, as in
hast (there is); **goft** (he said); **nist** (there isn't); **seft** (hard).
In general, throughout this book, the first time a word is used, it will be shown thus: colloquial or usual spoken form/literary or correct form. Thereafter the colloquial form will generally be used unless the style or sentence renders it necessary to do

otherwise. By correct or literary is meant the form as it is written down and which will not normally be used in ordinary speech, but which one will hear if things are being read out, on radio and television news, for example. In explanations of grammatical points, the correct forms will also be used. The glossaries will show the correct form.

■ Pronunciation Exercise

r   rāst (right); dorost (correct); rāh (way); barādar (brother)

<u>kh</u>   <u>kh</u>āhar (sister); ā<u>kh</u>ar (last); kā<u>kh</u> (palace); nimro<u>kh</u> (profile); e<u>kh</u>tiyār (will)

<u>sh</u>   <u>sh</u>ahr (town); <u>sh</u>eno (swimming); <u>sh</u>otor (camel); ā<u>sh</u> (broth)

<u>ch</u>   <u>ch</u>erā (why?); <u>ch</u>atr (umbrella); ā<u>ch</u>ār (spanner); mā<u>ch</u> (kiss); nu<u>ch</u> (sticky)

<u>zh</u>   ne<u>zh</u>ād (race); mo<u>zh</u>e (eyelash); <u>Zh</u>āle (a girl's name)

<u>gh</u>   <u>gh</u>arb (west); ta<u>gh</u>riban (approximately); o<u>gh</u>āb (eagle); a<u>gh</u>rab (scorpion); me<u>gh</u>dār (quantity); doru<u>gh</u> (lie); ma<u>gh</u>lub (defeated); <u>gh</u>ad (height); ān<u>gh</u>adr (that much)

'   sā'at (time); etā'at (obedience); ta'mir (repair); fe'lan (for the time being); jor'at (courage) e'terāz (protest); e'tebār (credit); rob' (quarter)

zh   ezhār (statement)

sh   eshāgh (Isaac); eshāl (diarrhoea)

■ Pronunciation Exercise: Doubled Consonants

pp   tappe (hill); lappe (yellow split peas)

jj   najjār (carpenter)

tt   ettefāgh (happening); ettehād (unity)

<u>chch</u> ba<u>chch</u>e (child)

vv   dovvom (second)

rr   <u>kh</u>arrāt (woodcarver)

yy   <u>kh</u>ayyāt (dressmaker, tailor)

CAPITAL LETTERS AND PUNCTUATION

Persian is written from right to left using the Arabic script. The Persian alphabet has four additional letters that represent sounds that do not exist in Arabic. In transcription these are **p, ch, g** and **zh**. The letters of the alphabet change their shape according to the position they occupy in the word, but capitalisation as such does not occur. The transcription used in this book, therefore, does not use capital letters either. Exception has been made in the case of proper nouns in the reading passages as it is felt that this will make things easier for the student.

Punctuation marks were not traditionally used in Persian as the sentence structure really renders them unnecessary. They are, however, now taught in schools and used in modern Persian, though in a much more limited way than in English, and this has been incorporated in the transcription.

Lesson One
(darse avval)

Read aloud:

■ 1. dar bāz-e/bāz ast   The door is open
2. panjere bast-ast/baste ast   The window is closed
3. havā garm-e/garm ast   The weather is hot
4. āb sard-e/sard ast   The water is cold
5. nun/nān tāz-ast/tāze ast   The bread is fresh
6. mādar mehrabun-e/mehrabān ast   The mother is loving
7. pedar khast-ast/khaste ast   The father is tired
8. pedarbozorg pir-e/pir ast   The grandfather is old
9. zan javun-e/javān ast   The woman is young
10. mādarbozorg mariz-e/mariz ast   The grandmother is ill
11. pesar sheîtun-e/sheîtān ast   The boy is mischievous
12. dokhtar kuchik-e/kuchak ast   The girl is small
13. khune/khāne bozorg-e/ast   The house is big
14. āb sard nist   The water is not cold
15. havā garm nist   The weather isn't hot
16. mard pir nist   The man is not old
17. ghazā khub-e/ast   The food is good
18. otobus por-e/ast   The bus is full
19. otāgh khāli-e/ast   The room is empty
20. otāgh tamiz nist   The room isn't clean

Vocabulary:

āb	water	chiz	thing
-e/ast	is	dar	door
bad	bad	dokhtar	girl/daughter
baste	closed	garm	warm
bāz	open	ghazā	food
bozorg	big	havā	weather
cherā	why	javun/ javān	young
che	what?	khāli	empty

khaste	tired	**otāgh**	room
khune/khāne	house	**otobus**	bus
khub	good	**panjere**	window
kojā	where?	**pedar**	father
kuchik/kuchak	small	**pesar**	boy/son
mādar	mother	**pir**	old
mard	man	**sard**	cold
mariz	ill	**sandali**	chair
mehrabun/	loving, kind	**sheîtun/**	mischievous
mehrabān		**sheîtān**	
miz	table	**tāze**	fresh
nun/nān	bread	**yā**	or
nist	is not, isn't	**yek**	one
o/va	and	**zan**	woman

Note:

	mādar	mother
	pedar	father
	bozorg	big
	madārbozorg	grandmother
	pedarbozorg	grandfather
but:	**nave**	grandson/granddaughter

ARTICLES

Persian has no articles as such:

khune	– house, the house
pedar	– father, the father

In a sentence, the noun on its own generally conveys the meaning of the definite article:

khune bozorg-e	– The house is big
pedar pir-e	– The father is old

The indefinite is expressed by the addition of an unaccented **i** at the end of the noun except where the noun ends with an **i**, in which case no distinction is made:

khunei	– a house
pedari	– a father
BUT **sandali**	– the chair/a chair

In colloquial usage, this **i** is largely replaced by the use of **yek** ('one') before the noun:

> **yek khune** – a house (one house)

yek tends to get further shortened in speech to **ye**, so you will hear:

ye <u>kh</u>une	– a house
ye ketāb	– a book
ye otā<u>gh</u>	– a room
ye tāksi	– a taxi
ye miz	– a table
ye sandali	– a chair
ye magas	– a fly
ye nafar	– a person (someone)

GENDER

As in English, nouns in Persian do not have a specific gender beyond that indicated in their meaning:

pesar <u>sh</u>êitun-e	– The boy is mischievous
do<u>kh</u>tar <u>kh</u>ub-e	– The girl is good
pedarbozorg pir-e	– The grandfather is old
mādarbozorg mariz-e	– The grandmother is ill
sandali bozorg-e	– The chair is big
miz bozorg-e	– The table is big
otā<u>gh</u> bozorg-e	– The room is big

-E/AST; HAST; NIST

-e/ast = is   **hast** = there is

The third person singular of the short form of the verb 'to be' (see Lesson Three) is **ast** or **hast**.

In spoken Persian **ast** is shortened to **e** after a word ending in a consonant, and is transcribed as **-e** in this book to help distinguish it from other **e** endings.

After a vowel, **ast** is shortened to **st** and transcribed **-st**. Where a word ends in **e** after a consonant, however, such as **baste** (closed), **tāze** (fresh), then **ast** is not shortened. The **e** of the word is elided instead and will be shown by a hyphen:

dar bast-ast (*dar baste ast*) – The door is closed

nun tāz-ast (*nun tāze ast*) – The bread is fresh

Ast and **hast** are not interchangeable and their correct use will best be learnt by examples and observation.

As a general rule, **hast** (*a*) conveys the idea of 'there is', or (*b*) is more emphatic than **ast**, depending on the context:

hotel <u>kh</u>ub-e/<u>kh</u>ub ast	– The hotel is good
nun hast	– There *is* bread

hast will also be used to ask 'is there?' (any bread, a room etc.):

nun hast?	– Is there any bread?

(See 'Interrogatives' below)

The negative of both **ast** and **hast** is **nist** – see sentence 14 at the beginning of this lesson.

WORD ORDER

Look again at the examples under the heading GENDER. Notice that the verb (**-e**) is at the end of the sentence or phrase. The usual word order in Persian is: subject – object (direct, then indirect) – verb. The verb normally comes at the end of the sentence, e.g.:

		verb	
miz	bozorg	-e (ast)	– The table is big
pesar	shêitun	-e (ast)	– The boy is naughty
do<u>kh</u>tar	<u>kh</u>ub	-e (ast)	– The girl is good

PLURALS

1. As a general rule and particularly in colloquial use, the plural of nouns is formed by the addition of the suffix -**hā**, which then carries the stress:

miz	– miz̄hā	(table, tables)
sandali	– sandalihā	(chair, chairs)
panjere	– panjerehā	(window, windows)
otobus	– otobushā	(bus, buses)
tāksi	– tāksihā	(taxi, taxis)

Note: In colloquial usage, in fact in speech in general, as opposed to the written word, the **h** of -**hā** is often not pronounced except when the word itself ends in the sound **e**:

   otobusā   tāksiā BUT panjerehā

2. The suffix -ān is used to form the plural of nouns denoting people, animals, birds etc.

For euphony, such nouns ending in o or u will also add v, those in a will add y and those in e will add g before the suffix:

mard	– mardān	(man, men)
zan	– zanān	(woman, women)
pedar	– pedarān	(father, fathers)
āghā	– āghāyān	(gentleman, gentlemen)
shenavande	– shenavandegān	(listener, listeners)
gusfand	– gusfandān	(one sheep, sheep)
morgh	– morghān	(chicken, chickens)
parande	– parandegān	(bird, birds)

The plural suffix -ān is not interchangeable with -hā, but most words, such as mādar, pedar, for which the correct, grammatical plurals are mādarān, pedarān, do in fact take -hā to form the plural in colloquial usage:

> madarhā (coll. mādarā)
> pedarhā (pedarā)
> pesarā
> dokhtarā

This is the form we will use most in this book, but do not expect even this to be entirely consistent. A common example of the inconsistencies that you will encounter is in the phrase 'ladies and gentlemen' – khānumhā va āghāyān, which shows the two different forms of the plural which are in use. khānum is the everyday word for 'lady' or 'Mrs', and is always khānumhā in the plural, whereas āghāyān is the correct grammatical plural of āghā.

3. The Arabic plural suffix -āt is also used, but not colloquially:
bāgh – bāghāt (garden, gardens)
A form of broken plural is also used:
> manzel – manāzel (house, houses)

But for both these examples and many others like them, bāghhā and manzelhā are more common in colloquial usage. The other forms are mentioned so that you may recognize them for what they are should you encounter them.

4. Use of the singular and plural:

There are two points of difference to be noted here between Persian and English:

(*a*) Persian uses the singular when considering the noun collectively or in a general sense:

Flies are dirty	– magas kasif-e
Books are good	– ketāb <u>kh</u>ub-e

(*b*) The singular is also used after numbers and after the word **chand** 'how many?':

five books	– panj ketāb
six boys	– <u>shish</u> pesar
how many books?	– <u>ch</u>and ketāb?

INTERROGATIVES

Questions are asked either with the use of interrogative words which are usually placed immediately before the verb or the noun to which they refer, or, in the absence of any interrogative word, by raising the tone of the voice towards the end of the sentence to indicate a question. The chief interrogative words are:

kojā	where?	ku	where?
<u>ch</u>i	what?	<u>ch</u>e	what?
<u>ch</u>erā	why?	<u>ch</u>e jur	how?
ki	who?	<u>ch</u>and	how many? (+
kudum/kodām	which?		*noun in singu-*
kêi	when?		*lar*)
<u>ch</u>etowr	how?		

■ havā <u>ch</u>etowr-e? — What's the weather like?

hotel kojā-st? (*kojā ast*) — Where is the hotel?

kudum hotel? — Which hotel?

ki-e (*pronounced* kiye)? — Who is it? (*e.g. when answering the door, though it is more polite to say* **bale**)

nun hast? — Is there any bread?

Note that **kojā ast** (where is?) is always contracted to **kojā-st** and **ki ast** (who is?) is always shortened to **ki-st** (*coll.* **ki-e**, *pronounced* ki-ye).

In colloquial use, the noun following the interrogative word **che** takes the indefinite suffix **-i** and as well as just 'what', **che** can also mean 'what sort of':

■ **che ketābi?** – What sort of book?/What book?

The word **āyā**, which is placed at the beginning of a sentence, is used to indicate that a question follows, but this is not colloquial and is seldom used in ordinary speech.

AND

The word for 'and' is **va**, usually shortened in speech to **o** (**vo** after a word ending in a vowel):

zan o mard – man and woman
pir o javun – young and old
pesar o dokhtar – boy and girl
pesarā vo dokhtarā – boys and girls
bozorg o kuchik – big and little
namak o felfel – salt and pepper
(Note the order in the first two phrases which is different from that used in English).

■ PHRASES AND EXPRESSIONS

salām (*or, more formal and less universal*, **salām alêıkum**)

Hello, How do you do?, *general greeting – used where we would say either* good morning, good afternoon *or* good evening. *The simple answer to* **salām** *is also* **salām**. *You will also hear* **alêıkum assalām**.

hāle shomā chetowr-e?
How are you?

khubam, mersi
I am well, thank you

sob bekhêır
Good morning (*less colloquial than just* **salām**)

khodāfez/khodā hāfez
Goodbye (*lit.* God, the Keeper)

shab bekhêır
Good night (*on going to bed, or also used in conjunction with*

<u>khodā</u> hāfez *on taking leave of*
someone at night)

bale	Yes
na	No
khêɪr	No (*more formal*)
nakhêɪr	*Emphatic no, i.e.* certainly not
khêɪlekhob	All right, O.K. (*Properly speaking this is* <u>khêɪli</u> <u>khub</u> – *very good*)

EXERCISES

A. Put into Persian:
1. The food is good
2. The water is hot
3. The window is not open
4. Hello
5. How are you?
6. I am well, thank you
7. Goodbye
8. a house, a chair, a man
9. Where is the hotel?
10. Which hotel? The Esteghlal
11. Five books
12. The bread is fresh
13. Is the girl small?
14. The weather is not warm
15. The house isn't big
16. The water is cold
17. The mother isn't bad
18. fathers, windows, boys
19. young and old
20. Is the room clean?

B. Read aloud and translate:
1. nun tāze nist
2. havā garm-e
3. havā garm ast
4. pesar bozorg-e
5. miz kojā-st?
6. dar bāz-e
7. panjere bast-ast?
8. kudum panjere?
9. dokhtar <u>sh</u>êɪtun nist
10. mādarbozorg mariz-e
11. magas kasif-e
12. havā <u>ch</u>etowr-e?

Lesson Two
(darse dovvom)

Read aloud:
■ 1. in otāghe man-e
   2. forudgāhe Tehrān bozorg-e
   3. bāghe mā ghashang-e
   4. bilite havāpeimā khêili gerun-e/gerān ast
   5. behtarin hotele shahr kojā-st?
   6. istgāhe otobuse Shemrun/Shemrān kojā-st?
   7. Maryam az Fāteme khêili bozorgtar-e
   8. in chamedune shomā-st?
   9. na, un chamedun māle man-e
  10. ketābe man kuchiktar az ketābe Hasan-e
      kuchiktarin ketābam ruye miz-e
  11. fārsi az ingilisi āsuntar-e/āsāntar ast
      Tehrān bozorgtarin shahre Irān-e
  12. māshine man az māshine Hasan behtar-e
      māshine Hosein az hame behtar-e
  13. lebāse Fāteme az lebāse Maryam tamiztar-e
      lebāse Zahrā az hame tamiztar-e
  14. nune emruz tāzetar az nune diruz-e
      tāzetarin nun māle maghāzeye Akbar āghā-st
  15. Maryam az Ali bozorgtar-e
      Hasan az hame bozorgtar-e
  16. in nun az un tāzetar-e
  17. in kafsh az in yeki bozorgtar-e

Vocabulary:

āghā	mister, sir	**be**	to
āsun	easy	**behtar**	better
az	than, from	**bilit**	ticket
bāgh	garden	**chamedun**	suitcase
barādar	brother	**dir**	late
barāye	for	**diruz**	yesterday

emruz	today	**māle***	belonging to
fārsi	Persian	**māshin**	car
forudgāh	airport	**medād**	pencil
ghashang	lovely	**ruye**	on
havāpeîmā	aeroplane	**sarbāz**	soldier
in	this	**sefid**	white
ingilisi	English	**shahr**	town, city
injā	here	**shojā'**	brave
kafsh	shoe	**siāh**	black
kasif	dirty	**Shemrān/**	name of the
ketāb	book	**Shemrun**	northern part
khāhar	sister		of Tehran
kheîli	very	**tamiz**	clean
lebās	dress, clothes	**tappe**	hill
maghāze	shop	**un/ān**	that
man	I, me	**unjā/ānjā**	there

*See Lesson Nine (1)

Proper names:
Boys: Mohammad, Hasan, Hosein, Akbar, Ali, Rezā
Girls: Maryam, Fāteme, Zahrā, Shirin

SUBJECT PRONOUNS

The subject pronouns are as follows:

singular		*plural*	
man	(I)	**mā**	(we)
to	(you)	**shomā**	(you)
u	(he, she)	**ishān**	(they)

There are two points to be noted here:

(a) the subject pronouns are only used for persons, therefore the 3rd person **u**, **ishān** (he, she, they) cannot be used to denote inanimate objects. 'It' is expressed by the demonstrative pronoun **un** (*plural* **unhā**) or not separately at all, as the verb ending will indicate the subject of the verb.

(b) the 2nd person plural **shomā** (you) is generally used as the polite form of address between strangers, when children address adults, as a sign of respect, etc.

The singular form **to** (you) is used between friends, by children and young people among themselves, by adults addressing children or superiors addressing inferiors. The distinction here is similar to that between *tu* and *vous* in French. It is best to use **shomā** in all cases at first.

THE EZĀFE: e

The **ezāfe** is a final **e** sound, rather like a suffix, after a word ending in a consonant, or **ye** after a word ending in a vowel. It has several uses:

(a) *To express the possessive*:

khuneye pedar	–	the father's house (*lit.* house-of the father)
bilite otobus	–	the bus ticket (ticket-of the bus)
barādare Maryam	–	Mariam's brother
khāhare Hasan	–	Hassan's sister
dare khune	–	the door of the house
charkhe māshin	–	the wheel of the car
lebāse mard	–	the man's clothes
chādore zan	–	the woman's veil

Note the word order which is quite different from the English usage of 's which is what it conveys:

    khuneye mard – the house-of the man.

It is the thing which is possessed which takes the *ezāfe*, not the possessor, as in English.

(b) *When an adjective qualifies a noun* – again note the word order: noun + *ezāfe* – adjective:

hotele khub	–	the good hotel
lebāse tamiz	–	the clean dress
barādare bozorg	–	the big brother
farshe bozorg	–	the big carpet
nune tāze	–	the fresh bread

restorāne khub	– the good restaurant
daste rāst	– the right hand (*note: this can also mean* on the right)

If the noun is qualified by more than one adjective, the 'qualifying' *ezāfe* is also added to each adjective except the final one:

khuneye kuchike sefid	– the small white house
nune garme tāze	– the hot fresh bread
farshe bozorge gerun	– the large expensive carpet

If the noun is plural, then the *ezāfe* is added onto the plural ending and since this is generally **-hā**, the *ezāfe* will be **ye** and not **e**:

khunehāye bozorg	– large houses
bachchehāye kuchik	– small children

(c) *For possessive adjectives* – there are no separate possessive adjectives as such (my, your, their etc.) in Persian. The meaning 'my book', 'your book' etc. is rendered exactly as the possessive in (a) above, using the subject pronouns instead of the noun:

singular:	**ketābe man**	my book (*lit.* book-of I)
	ketābe to	your book (*familiar*)
	ketābe u	his/her book
plural:	**ketābe mā**	our book
	ketābe shomā	your book (*polite*)
	ketābe ishān	their book

Much more common, however, especially in speech, is the use of the pronominal suffixes:

-am	(my)	**-emān** (*coll.* **-emun**)	(our)
-at (*coll.* **-et**)	(your)	**-etān** (*coll.* **-etun**)	(your)
-ash (*coll.* **-esh**)	(his/her/ its)	**-eshān** (*coll.* **-eshun**)	(their)

The colloquial form for 'my book', 'your book', etc. will therefore be:

ketābam	my book	**ketābemun**	our book
ketābet	your book	**ketābetun**	your book
ketābesh	his/her/its book	**ketābeshun**	their book

likewise:

barādaram	barādaremun
barādaret	barādaretun
barādaresh	barādareshun

but where a word ends in a vowel, the formal pattern will be:

khune/khāne

khāneam	khāneyemān
khāneat	khāneyetān
khāneash	khāneyeshān

which is further shortened in speech to:

Where the noun qualified by the possessive adjective is also qualified by an adjective or adjectives, then the pronominal suffix is added to the final adjective:

For example	your brother – **barādaret/at**
but	your big brother – **barādare bozorget/at**
	your big, thin brother – **barādare bozorge lāgharet/at**
	your small naughty son – **pesare kuchike shêitunet/at**

ADJECTIVES

Adjectives remain unchanged whether the noun they qualify is singular or plural. As a general rule, they follow the nouns they qualify and the noun takes the *ezāfe* ending to relate it to the adjective:

    nune tāze – fresh bread
    nunhāye tāze – fresh bread(s)
    dokhtare bozorg – the big girl
    dokhtarhāye bozorg – the big girls
    marde pir – the old man
    mardhāye pir – old men
    sarbāze shojā' – the brave soldier
    sarbāzhāye shojā' – the brave soldiers

zane javun – the young woman
zanhāye javun – the young women

Departure from this rule is used for stylistic effect, in special expressions or ones which are much-used which will be pointed out as we encounter them. For example, **marde pir**, the old man, is often rendered as **piremard**, likewise **zane pir** becomes **pirezan**.

Notice that the above phrases are definite – *the* big girl, etc. Where the noun qualified by the adjective is indefinite, the indefinite suffix **i** is added to the *qualifying adjective*:

dokhtare bozorg	– the big girl
dokhtare bozorgi	– a big girl
marde pir	– the old man
marde piri	– an old man

If there is more than one adjective, the indefinite **i** is added to the last one:

farshe bozorge geruni – a large expensive carpet

The indefinite suffix **i** is never stressed.

COMPARISON OF ADJECTIVES

The comparative and superlative of adjectives are formed by the addition of the suffixes **-tar**, for the comparative, and **-tarin**, for the superlative, to the adjectives. 'Than' is rendered by the preposition **az**:
Thus:

Maryam az Fāteme kuchiktar-e – Maryam is smaller (*or* younger) than Fāteme

otobus az tāksi bozorgtar-e – The bus is bigger than the taxi

The comparative follows the noun:

khuneye bozorgtar	**nune tāzetar**
marde behtar	**pesare kuchiktar**
havāye sardtar	**māshine behtar**

but the superlative comes before the noun:

bozorgtarin khune	**tāzetarin nun**

behtarin mard	kuchiktarin pesar
sardtarin havā	behtarin māshin

Here are the comparative and superlatives of some of the more common adjectives:

garm	garmtar	garmtarin	(hot)
sard	sardtar	sardtarin	(cold)
bozorg	bozorgtar	bozorgtarin	(big)
kuchik	kuchiktar	kuchiktarin	(little)
sakht	sakhtar	sakhtarin	(difficult)
āsān/un	āsuntar	āsuntarin	(easy)
tāze	tāzetar	tāzetarin	(fresh, new)
kohne	kohnetar	kohnetarin	(old – of thing)
kutā	kutātar	kutātarin	(short)
boland	bolandtar	bolandtarin	(long, tall)
nazdik	nazdiktar	nazdiktarin	(near)
dur	durtar	durtarin	(far)
bad	badtar	badtarin	(bad)
khub	behtar	behtarin	(good)

Note: (a) **khub** changes its stem in the comparative and superlative, using the form **beh-**

   (b) **sakhtar** is, of course, **sakht-tar**, but the second 't' is dropped in speech. The combination 'dt' is also pronounced very close together.

   (c) when there is no point of comparison for the superlative, i.e. when we want to say 'the biggest' without specifying the biggest of which things, a very common way of expressing the superlative in Persian is by using the construction **az hame** (than all) + the comparative, e.g. **az hame bozorgtar**

   Maryam az hame behtar-e – Maryam is the best

DEMONSTRATIVES

The demonstrative pronouns are:

in	– this (one)	**inā/inhā**	– these (ones)
un/ān	– that (one), it	**unā/ānhā**	– those (ones), they

These pronouns may refer to either people or things:

in bozorg-e	–	this is big
un khub-e	–	that/it is good
inhā bozorg-and*	–	these (*people or things*) are big
unhā khub-and	–	those/they are good

Note: -and = are, and will be explained in Lesson Three.

If, therefore, we want to say 'this bread is fresher than that', we will say **in nun az un tāzetar-e**. Likewise:

in kafsh az un kuchiktar-e	– This shoe is smaller than that one
in otāgh az un behtar-e	– This room is better than that one

The demonstrative adjectives are also **in** and **un** but when used as such they do not vary in the plural:

in dar	– this door	**in darā/hā**	– these doors
un ketāb	– that book	**un ketābā/hā**	– those books
in khune	– this house	**in khunehā**	– these houses

■ PHRASES AND EXPRESSIONS

har che zudtar	– As soon as possible
che behtar	– So much the better
mesle in ke	– It looks as if, I think
besm ellāhe rahmāne rahim	– In the Name of God, the Compassionate, the Merciful. *This Arabic phrase should be learned and recognised for it is widely used – to begin prayers, speeches, letters, documents, etc.*
besmellā	– In the Name of God. *This is the short form of* **besm ellāhe rahmāne rahim** *and is generally used before starting anything. It is also widely used, in speech only, as a blessing upon an action to follow.*
mersi	– Thank you
khêili mamnun	– Thank you
bi zahmat	– Please (*lit.* without trouble)
lotfan	– Please

Note: In speaking Persian, even in colloquial usage, people are much more formally polite than is customary in English. There is therefore a much greater variety of polite phrases and expressions. These are covered in greater detail in Lesson Twelve.

EXERCISES

A. Put into Persian:
1. My house is bigger than Hassan's house
2. The biggest house is on the hill
3. My car is smaller than Hassan's car
4. Fateme's dress is cleaner than Maryam's
5. This dress is the cleanest
6. The hotel is clean
7. My room is small
8. This is your book
9. That table is dirty
10. That is my black suitcase

B. Read aloud and translate:
1. bilite shomā ruye miz-e
2. lebāse dokhtare bozorg sefid-e
3. mādare Maryam mariz-e
4. in dar bāz-e
5. un pesar sheitun-e
6. barādaram az hame behtar-e
7. tamiztarin hotel
8. chamedune man siāh-e
9. istgāhe otobus kojā-st?
10. behtarin hotele shahr kojā-st?

C. Put into Persian:
1. My book
2. My big book
3. Your house is small
4. His car is big
5. The garden door is open
6. The girl's dress is clean

7. My mother's room isn't big
8. Your father's car is small
9. My brother's house is on the hill
10. Hassan's sister is ill

D. *Read aloud, putting in the ezāfe:*
1. ketāb Hasan (*Hassan's book*)
2. khune mard (*the man's house*)
3. khāhar man (*my sister*)
4. khune man (*my house*)
5. barādar (*his/her brother*)
6. hotel khub (*the good hotel*)
7. bilit otobus (*the bus ticket*)
8. ye farsh bozorg (*a big carpet*)
9. ketāb shomā (*your book*)
10. charkh māshin (*the wheel of the car*)

Lesson Three
(darse sevvom)

Read aloud:
■ 1. havāpêimā dir resid/rasid. dustam unjā/anjā nabud. bā tāksi be
hotel raftam. khêili dur nabud. otāgham bozorg o tamiz bud.
sobune/sobhāne khordam. ba'd neshastam ye nāme neveshtam
o kami ruznāme khundam/khāndam. dustam bā māshinesh
umad/āmad. manzelesh nazdike hotel bud. bā ham be
manzelesh raftim.

2. bahār bud. derakhthā gharghe shokufe budand. sedāye gonji-
shkhā az hame taraf miumad. nasime molāyemi mivazid. bach-

<u>ch</u>ehā tuye ku<u>ch</u>e midowidand/midavidand. man tuye otā<u>gh</u>am budam o barāye dustam nāme mineve<u>sh</u>tam.

Vocabulary:

az	from	mineve<u>sh</u>tam	I was writing
bā	with	mivazid	it was blow-ing
ba'd	then		
ba<u>chch</u>ehā	children	molāyem	mild, gentle
bā ham	together	nabud	he was not
bahār	spring	nāme	letter
barāye	to	nasim	breeze
bud	was	nazdike	near (*prep.*)
budand	were	ne<u>sh</u>astam	I sat
dera<u>kh</u>thā	the trees	neve<u>sh</u>tam	I wrote
dur	far	raftam	I went
dust	friend	raftim	we went
gonji<u>sh</u>k	sparrow	resid	he/she/it arrived
<u>gh</u>ar<u>gh</u>e	covered in		
hame	all	ruznāme	newspaper
jā	place	sedā	sound, voice
kami	a little	sobune/	breakfast
<u>kh</u>ordam	I ate	sobhāne	
<u>kh</u>undam	I read	<u>sh</u>okufe	blossom
manzel	home, house	taraf	side
miāmad	he/she/it was coming	tuye	in (*prep.*)
		unjā/ānjā	there
midowidand	they were running		

Notes: nazdike and tuye are prepositions which take the *ezāfe* (see Lesson Six).

barāye usually means 'for', but it is more colloquial to say barāye dustam name mineve<u>sh</u>tam than be dustam . . . although be is the usual word for 'to'

VERBS I

A. THE INFINITIVE

The infinitives of all verbs end in **-dan**, **-tan** or **-idan** and each verb has two stems, the *present stem* and the *past stem*, which form the basis for the conjugation of the various tenses.

The infinitive itself can be used as a noun, e.g.:

rundan sakht-e	–	Driving is difficult
khordan āsun-e	–	Eating is easy

Taking the **-an** off the end of the infinitive will always give the past stem, and taking the **-dan**, **-tan** or **-idan** off will usually give the present stem, but as so many verbs have an irregular present stem, each new verb should be learnt as two elements: infinitive, from which the past stem is regularly formed, and the present stem. Once these two elements are known, the conjugation of almost any verb simply follows the rules. Each new verb will therefore be shown thus: infinitive (present stem) e.g. **rāndan (rān)**.
We shall take the verbs **raftan** (to go), **rāndan** (*coll.* **rundan**) (to drive) and **rasidan** (*coll.* **residan**) (to arrive) as models:

Infinitive	*Present stem*
raftan	**rav**
rundan	**run**
residan	**res**

B. TENSES FORMED FROM THE PAST STEM

1. The simple past (or preterite)

Since the past stem is closest to the infinitive, the natural order for learning the tenses in Persian begins with the simple past.
To form the simple past (I went, I drove, I arrived etc.), we start with the infinitive. If we take the **-an** ending off this, we are left with the past stem:

raftan (to go)	– **raft**
randan (to drive)	– **rand**
residan (to arrive)	– **resid**

To this we add the personal endings

	Singular		Plural	
1st person	**-am**	(I)	**-im**	(we)
2nd person	**-i**	(you)	**-id**	(you)
3rd person	–	(he/she/it)	**-and**	(they)

The simple past is therefore:

	Singular		Plural	
1st person:	**raftam**	(I went)	**raftim**	(we went)
2nd person:	**rafti**	(you went)	**raftid**	(you went)
3rd person:	**raft**	(he/she/it went)	**raftand**	(they went)

Note: The stress is on the syllable before the personal ending, and not on the ending itself. '**and**' is generally pronounced '**an**'.

Likewise:

rundam	(I drove)	**rundim**	(we drove)
rundi	(you drove)	**rundid**	(you drove)
rund	(he/she/it drove)	**rundand**	(they drove)
residam	(I arrived)	**residim**	(we arrived)
residi	(you arrived)	**residid**	(you arrived)
resid	(he/she/it arrived)	**residand**	(they arrived)

The simple past of all verbs is formed in this way.

Note that because the personal endings already indicate who is doing the action, the subject pronouns are not used in simple sentences:

e.g.	**be madrese raft**	–	He/she went to school
	az madrese āmad	–	He/she came from school
	be edāre raftam	–	I went to the office
	az edāre āmadim	–	We came from the office

When, however, the idea of *who* is doing an action is to be stressed or contrasted or reinforced in some way, then the subject pronouns are used as well:

e.g. **u be madrese raft ammā barādaresh dar khune mund/mānd**
He/she went to school but his/her brother stayed at home
(**māndan/mundan** = to stay; *present stem*: **mān/mun**)

mā az edāre āmadim ammā unhā mundand
We left (came from) the office but they stayed

If the subject is a proper noun, the verb still carries the personal ending:

Hasan be madrese raft	– Hassan went to school
Maryam o Hasan be	– Mariam and Hassan
madrese raftand	went to school

The negative is formed by adding the verbal prefix **na-** to the beginning of the simple past; the negative prefix then carries the stress:

naraftam (I did not go)
narafti (you did not go)
narundam (I did not drive)
narundi (you did not drive)
naresidam (I did not arrive)

Here are a few more examples of the infinitive and the past stem:

gereftan	**gereft**	to take
āmadan	**āmad**	to come
dādan	**dād**	to give
kharidan	**kharid**	to buy
khordan	**khord**	to eat
neshastan	**neshast**	to sit
khundan	**khund**	to read
neveshtan	**nevesht**	to write
shodan	**shod**	to become

The most common use of the simple past is to express a completed action in the past. It is also the narrative tense – i.e. the tense used to describe or report on actions which have taken place.

Note also the following use of the simple past for an action which is about to be completed:

āmadam	– I'm coming (*in answer to* 'hurry up', *or* 'are you coming?')

raftim .– We're off, we're going

In both the above examples, the simple past is being used in response to questions or commands which imply that the action is overdue and ought already to have taken place. The answer to a straightforward question 'are you coming?' would be in the present tense as in English.

2. *The imperfect*

The imperfect is formed by the addition of the verbal prefix **mi-** to the simple past, with the stress on this prefix:

miraftam	(I was going)	**miraftim**	(we were going)
mirafti		**miraftid**	
miraft		**miraftand**	

mirundam	(I was driving)	**mirundim**	
mirundi		**mirundid**	
mirund		**mirundand**	

miresidam	(I was arriving)	**miresidim**	
miresidi		**miresidid**	
miresid		**miresidand**	

The imperfect is used to express continuous, habitual or recurrent actions in the past:

e.g. **pedaram har ruz be edāre miraft**
My father used to go to the office every day
Fāteme har ruz az madrese miāmad
Fateme used to come from school every day
man hamishe be masjed miraftam
I always went to the mosque
Hasan har ruz az edāre miāmad
Hassan came from the office every day
Maryam nun mipokht
Mariam was baking bread
monshi nāme mineyesht
The secretary was writing a letter

The imperfect is also used in certain kinds of conditional sentences (See Lesson Ten).

In the imperfect tense, the negative prefix is **ne-** and the stress is transferred to this prefix:

nemiraftam	(I was not going)
nemirafti	(you were not going)
nemirundam	(I was not driving)
nemirundi	(you were not driving)

3. The past participle

The past participle consists of the past stem plus an **e** on the end which carries the stress, and this will be transcribed thus: **é** for the sake of differentiation:

raftan	**raft**	**rafté**
rundan	**rund**	**rundé**
residan	**resid**	**residé**

It is used in the formation of the compound tenses (perfect and pluperfect) which will be covered in Lesson Five. It is also used adjectivally.

C. The verb 'to be'

(*a*) We have already encountered the use of **ast**, shortened to **-e** or **-st**, meaning 'is' (Lesson One). In fact the verb 'to be' has two forms in Persian. The present tense is always expressed:
(i) by the use of the following personal endings which are added to the preceding word (except in the case of the 3rd person singular where **ast** stands on its own) and can also be called the short form of 'to be'.

Singular		*Plural*	
-am	(I am)	**-im**	(we are)
-i	(you are)	**-id**	(you are)
ast/-e	(he/she/it is)	**-and**	(they are)

Thus:

khub	(good)		
khubam	(I am good)	**khubim**	(we are good)
khubi	(you are good)	**khubid**	(you are good)
khub ast/-e	(he/she/it is good)	**khuband**	(they are good)

If one remembers the basic rule about word order – i.e. subject, object, verb, then it will not be difficult to decide where to put these endings.

Some examples of the use of the short form for 'to be':

barādaram kuchik-e	–	My brother is little
dustam mariz-e	–	My friend is sick
dar bāz-e	–	The door is open
ketāb ruye miz-e	–	The book is on the table
nāhār hāzer-e	–	Lunch is ready
shām hāzer-e	–	Supper is ready
man tuye hamum-am	–	I am in the bath
pesarā sheîtun-and	–	The boys are naughty

Note, however, the two colloquialisms:

gorosnam-e	–	I am hungry
teshnam-e	–	I am thirsty

gorosne means 'hungry' and teshne means 'thirsty', therefore the correct form should in fact be gorosne-am, teshne-am, but these have been contracted to gorosnam, teshnam and then had the 3rd person singular -e added also.

(ii) by the use of the more emphatic form hast, also referred to in Lesson One, which is conjugated as follows (remember, the personal endings do not take the stress):

hastam	hastim
hasti	hastid
hast	hastand

The form in (i) above is much more common in colloquial use to express the simple present tense of 'to be', hast having the slightly more emphatic meaning already explained, *but* hast etc. is normally used after a word ending in i, e.g.:

ingilisi hastid?	–	Are you English?
khāreji hastid?	–	Are you a foreigner? (*lit*. are you foreign?)

Both these forms survive in the present tense only, and although the infinitives astan or hastan are to be found in Persian dictionaries and grammar books, they are no longer fully conjugated.

A plural subject denoting rational beings takes a plural verb, but inanimate objects and irrational beings take the singular:

e.g.
bachchehā injā hastand	– The children are here
khāhar o barādaram dar Tabriz-and	– My brother and sister are in Tabriz
ketābā injā nist	– The books aren't here
ruznāmehā injā-st	– The newspapers are here
kafshā hāzer nist	– The shoes aren't ready

For the negative in both cases the negative of **hast** is used:

nistam	(I am not)	**nistim**	(we are not)
nisti	(you are not)	**nistid**	(you are not)
nist	(he/she/it is not)	**nistand**	(they are not)

(b) All other tenses of the verb 'to be' are expressed by the verb **budan** (**bāsh**) which is conjugated as follows:

Preterite/simple past

budam	(I was)	**budim**	(we were)
budi	(you were)	**budid**	(you were)
bud	(he/she/it was)	**budand**	(they were)

As with the preterite of other verbs, the negative prefix is **na-** which is stressed:

   nabudam, nabudi, etc.

Imperfect

The forms **mibudam, mibudi** etc. are regularly formed but seldom used except in certain kinds of conditional sentences and not at all in colloquial speech. These are literary and only given here for the purpose of recognition should you encounter them.

Present tense

This is formed quite regularly from the present stem (**bāsh**),

mibāsham	**mibāshim**
mibāshi	**mibāshid**
mibāshad	**mibāshand**

but it is not normally used to express 'I am', 'you are' etc. It is in fact so rarely used as such that if you ask the average Iranian the present tense of **budan**, you will probably be told **hastam, hasti, hast** etc.

PHRASES AND EXPRESSIONS

inshāllā/enshā allāh	God willing. *A much-used phrase in reference to future time.*
māshāllā	*lit.* what God wills; *a much used verbal talisman. It is always said if one has paid someone a compliment, or praised something. It's very much like 'touch wood' only with a religious element.* **dast be chub** *is also said ('touch wood'), but not as much.*
āftāb bud	The sun was shining
bārun gereft	It started to rain
dorost shod	*lit.* it came right; *said of a satisfactory outcome*
khub shod/bad shod	It turned out well/badly
kharāb shod	It was spoilt, it went wrong

EXERCISES

A. Read aloud and then translate:
1. otāgham bozorg o tamiz bud
2. dustam az edāre āmad
3. Maryam subune khord
4. manzele dustam dur nabud
5. ingilisi hastid?
6. otobus por bud
7. tāksi khāli bud
8. Hasan har ruz be edāre miraft
9. neshestam o kami ruznāme khundam
10. bā dustesh be hotel raft
11. cherā āmadi?
12. nasime molāyemi mivazid

B. Put into Persian:
1. The plane arrived late
2. My room was large and clean
3. My friend was there
4. We came yesterday
5. The secretary was writing a letter
6. Did you write a letter?
7. Is your daughter's school there?
8. Did you go to his house?

C. Make the sentences in exercise B negative

Lesson Four
(darse chaharom)

Note: Passage 1 is a little conversation and to preserve the flow
and feeling of the text, the usual colloquial/literary format
has not been followed. It is given instead in the vocabulary.
Read aloud:

■ 1. kojā miri?
mikhām beram mive bekharam
manam bāhet miām
pas zud bāsh chun ziād vaght nadāram
piāde miri?
bale

■ 2. Maryam har ruz be maghāzeye Akbar āghā mire/miravad. da
unjā chāi o shir o kare vo panir mikhare/mikharad. ba'd b
nunvāi mire vo nun mikhare. diruz az ghassābi gusht kharic
emruz unjā nemire. mire davākhune barāye dokhtares
davā mikhare. ba'd be manzelesh mire vo be back
chehāsh/bachchehāyash sobune mide/midahad.

Vocabulary:

bāhet/bā to	with you	**mide/midahad**	he/she/it gives
bā<u>sh</u>	be!	**mi<u>kh</u>ām/**	I want
	(*imperative*)	**mi<u>kh</u>āham**	
be	to	**mi<u>kh</u>are/**	he/she buys
be<u>kh</u>aram	that I may buy	**mi<u>kh</u>arad**	
beram	that I may go	**miri/miravi**	you go
<u>ch</u>āi	tea	**mire/miravad**	he/she goes
<u>ch</u>un	because	**mive**	fruit
davā	medicine	**nadāram**	I haven't got
davā<u>kh</u>une	pharmacy	**nemire**	she doesn't
dar (*prep.*)	in		go
gu<u>sh</u>t	meat	**nunvāi**	bakery
<u>gh</u>assābi	butcher's	**panir**	cheese
har	each, every	**piāde**	on foot
kare	butter	**<u>sh</u>ir**	milk
<u>kh</u>arid	he/she bought	**va<u>gh</u>t**	time
kojā	where?	**ziād**	a lot
ma<u>gh</u>āze	shop	**zud**	early
manam/man	me too	**zud bā<u>sh</u>**	be quick
ham			

Note: **bāhet**: colloquial form of **bā to** (with you)

manam: colloquial form of **man ham** (me too, I also)

VERBS II

TENSES FORMED FROM THE PRESENT STEM

1. The present tense

The present tense is formed by the addition of the verbal prefix **mi-** to the *present stem*, followed by the personal endings which are the same as for the simple past, except for the third person singular which is **-ad**. The endings will therefore be:

	Singular	Plural
1st person:	**-am**	**-im**
2nd person:	**-i**	**-id**
3rd person:	**-ad**	**-and**

In regular verbs, if we take the **-dan**, **-tan** or **-idan** off the infinitive, we will be left with the present stem, but as already mentioned in Lesson Three, many verbs have an irregular present stem which is why this should be learnt with each new verb.

The present stem of **raftan** is **rav**, of **rundan**, **run**, of **residan**, **res**, therefore:

> **mi + rav + am = miravam** (I go)
> **mi + run + am = mirunam** (I drive)
> **mi + res + am = miresam** (I arrive)

As with the imperfect, the stress is on the verbal prefix **mi-**.

From **raftan** (**rav**), we will therefore have:

miravam	(I go)	**miravim**	(we go)
miravi	(you go)	**miravid**	(you go)
miravad	(he/she/it goes)	**miravand**	(they go)

from **rundan** (**run**):

mirunam	(I drive)	**mirunim**	(we drive)
miruni	(you drive)	**mirunid**	(you drive)
mirunad	(he/she/it drives)	**mirunand**	(they drive)

from **residan** (**res**):

miresam	(I arrive)	**miresim**	(we arrive)
miresi		**miresid**	
miresad		**miresand**	

In speech, the **-ad** ending of the 3rd person singular of all verbs formed from the present stem is shortened to **-e** when the stem ends in a consonant. Therefore:

miresad becomes **mirese** (he/she/it arrives *or* is arriving)
mirunad becomes **mirune** (he/she drives *or* is driving)

When the present stem ends in **h**, **v**, or a vowel, however, (*a*) a **y** is sometimes inserted after the vowel and (*b*) tenses formed from it are contracted still further. These have to be learned individually as there is no general rule to indicate when this takes place.

(i) **raftan** – present stem: **rav**
    miravam, miravi, miravad, etc become:

miram	**mirim**
miri	**mirid**
mire	**miran**

(ii) **āmadan (ā)** – to come
    miāyam, miāi, miāyad, miāim, miāid, miāyand, become

miām	**miāim**
miāy	**miāid**
miād	**miān**

(iii) **dādan (deh)** – to give; literary form: **midaham, midahi** etc.

(Note the exceptional change of the vowel **e** to **a** when the verb is conjugated)

midam	**midim**
midi	**midid**
mide	**midan**

The stress remains on the first syllable.

The negative is formed by adding the prefix **ne-**, which then carries the stress: e.g.

nemiram, nemiri, nemire etc

The present tense in Persian renders both the simple present and the present continuous in English.

Hasan miād (*miāyad*)	–	Hassan comes/is coming
Maryam mire	–	Mariam goes/is going
barf miād	–	It snows/is snowing
Maryam māshin mirune	–	Mariam drives a car/is driving
monshi nāme minevise	–	The secretary writes/is writing a letter
bārun nemiād	–	It doesn't rain/isn't raining

It is also used for an action which began in the past and continues into the present:

panj ruz-e ke dar hotel-am – I have been in the hotel for five
days (and am still there)

(*Note:* **ke** = 'that' *and will be covered more fully in Lesson Ten*)

az diruz tā hālā minevise – He has been writing since yesterday

In colloquial usage, the present is also used for the *future*:

e.g. **fardā bilit mikharam** – I'll buy a ticket tomorrow

It will always be clear from the context whether or not the future
tense is meant.

2. *The Subjunctive*

The subjunctive is formed from the present stem with the addition
of the prefix **be-** and the personal endings. Otherwise it follows the
same pattern as the present:

be + present stem + personal endings = subjunctive

e.g. **rundan** – (**run**):

berunam	(that I may drive)	**berunim**
beruni		**berunid**
berune/ad		**berunand**

raftan – (**rav**):

beravam	(that I may go)	**beravim**
beravi		**beravid**
beravad		**beravand**

which will be shortened in speech to:

beram	**berim**
beri	**berid**
bere	**berand**

Note that the subjunctive of **budan** (**bāsh**), 'to be', is formed from
the present stem plus the personal endings but *without* the **be-**:

bāsham	**bāshim**
bāshi	**bāshid**
bāshe/-ad	**bāshand**

The present subjunctive is used a great deal in Persian. Here are some of its uses:

(i) The first and third persons singular and plural are used in questions which are expressed in English by 'shall I/we?' etc.:

beram khune?	–	Shall I go home?
berim bāzār?	–	Shall we go to the bazaar?
berim sheno?	–	Shall we go swimming?
bere kharid?	–	Shall he/she go shopping?

(ii) The first person plural is used in the sense of 'let's':

berim khune	Let's go home
berim bāzār	Let's go to the bazaar
berim sheno	Let's go swimming

(iii) The subjunctive is always used after the verbs:

khāstan (khāh)	– to want
and **tavānestan (tavān)**	– to be able

mikhām māshin berunam – I want to drive a car
mitunam māshin berunam – I can drive a car

In each case both **khāstan** and **tavānestan** and the verb expressing the action agree with each other in person and number, and this usage should be noted as it is quite unlike English:

mikhām (*1st pers. sing. present*) **beram** (*1st pers. sing. subjunctive*)

I want (*1st pers. sing. present*) to go (*infinitive*)

mikhām beram bāzār	– I want to go to the bazaar
mikhād bere khune	– He wants to go home
mikhām beram mive bekharam	– I want to go and buy some fruit

In order to say 'I do not want to go', 'I cannot drive' etc, the stressed negative prefix **ne-** is put before the appropriate form of **khāstan** or **tavānestan**:

nemikhām beram	– I don't want to go
nemitune berune	– He can't drive

(iv) The words **bāyad** (must, ought to) and **s̲h̲āyad** (perhaps, maybe) also take the present subjunctive when referring to the present or future:

bāyad beram k̲h̲une	– I must go home
bāyad kafs̲h̲ bek̲h̲aram	– I must buy some shoes
s̲h̲āyad beram mosāferat	– Perhaps I will go away (on a journey)
s̲h̲āyad manzel bās̲h̲e	– Maybe he's at home

(v) Whenever the verb **gozās̲h̲tan (gozār)** which also means 'to put' is used in the sense of 'to permit', 'to allow', the verb following it is in the subjunctive:

(Note that in spoken Persian, the **go** is also dropped from the present stem of **gozās̲h̲tan** so that tenses formed from it sound as though the stem were **zār**.)

bezār beram	– Let me go
bezār bebinam	– Let me see
nemizāram beri	– I won't let you go

(vi) The subjunctive is used in a variety of subordinate clauses which will be covered in Lesson Ten.

3. The imperative

The imperative singular is formed by adding the prefix **be-** to the present stem:

rundan (run)	– **berun**	– drive!
residan (res)	– **beres**	– arrive! (get there!)

The following exceptions should, however, be noted:

(*a*) If the present stem ends in **av**, this becomes **o** in the imperative singular:

s̲h̲enidan (s̲h̲enav) → **bes̲h̲eno** →**bes̲h̲no** (hear!)

(*b*) If the imperative singular ends in **o**, the prefix **be-** sometimes becomes **bo-**:

raftan (rav) → **bero** → **boro** (go!)
These cases have to be learned individually.

(c)   The verb **budan** does not take **be-**:

budan (bāsh) → **bāsh**

The plural takes the **-id** ending of the second person plural:

berunid   beresid   berid   bāshid

The negative imperative, 'do not . .' is formed by the use of the prefix **na-** instead of **be/bo-**:

narun	–	**narunid**
nares	–	**naresid**
naro	–	**narid**
nabāsh	–	**nabāshid**

Apart from the actual numerical plural sense, i.e. for commands to more than one person, the imperative plural is also the more polite form when addressing a single person in the same way as **shomā** (see Lesson Two, Subject Pronouns (b)).

NOUN OF THE AGENT

A noun denoting the person doing the action concerned and therefore called the *noun of the agent* is formed from the present stem of some verbs.

This is done by adding the suffix **-ande** to the present stem. A point to notice here is that the vowel changes that take place in the other spoken forms of such verbs do not usually apply to the noun of the agent.

e.g. **rāndan (rān)** – to drive: **rānande** – driver (*pl.* **rānandehā**)
forukhtan (forush) – to sell: **forushande** – salesperson (*pl.* **forushandehā**)
khāndan – (**khān**) – to read, to sing: **khānande** – reader, singer (*pl.* **khānandehā**)
shenidan – (**shenav**) – to hear: **shenavande** – hearer, listener (*pl.* **shenavandegān**)

Some common verbs:

āmadan (ā)	to come
bordan (bar)	to take
āvardan (ār) (*coll.* āvordan)	to bring
goftan (gu)	to say
budan (bāsh)	to be
shodan (shav)	to become
kardan (kon)	to do
dādan (deh)	to give
gereftan (gir)	to take
khāndan (khān) (*coll.* khundan)	to read
bastan (band)	to close, to shut
neshastan (neshin)	to sit
istādan (ist)	to stand, to stop
didan (bin)	to see
shenidan (sheno)	to hear
khordan (khor)	to eat/drink
khābidan (khāb)	to sleep
nushidan (nush)	to drink
dāshtan (dār)	to have
zadan (zan)	to hit

Notes:

1. Strictly speaking, **khordan** means 'to eat', but it is also generally used to mean 'to drink':

   e.g. ghazā khordam   –   I ate food
   āb khordam   –   I drank water

   In fact, the term for 'drinking-water' is **ābe khordan**.

2. **nushidan** is seldom used in colloquial speech, but the noun derived from it **nushābe** is commonly used to refer to non-alcoholic drinks of the bottled fizzy kind which are available in variety and very popular.

   Thus in a restaurant or even in a shop one might ask:
   nushābe chi dārid? – What do you have in the way of drinks?

   or one might be asked:

   nushābe chi mikhāid – What drink would you like?

3. The verb **dāshtan** does not take **mi-** or **be-**. Its present tense is:

singular	*plural*
dāram (I have)	**dārim**
dāri	**dārid**
dāre/ad	**dārand**

The imperfect is the same as the simple past:

dāshtam: I had, I was having

The present subjunctive is:

dāshté bāsham
dāshté bāshi etc.

which is also the form of the past subjunctive (see Lesson Five).

The imperative of **dāshtan** is **dāshté bāsh**.

■ PHRASES AND EXPRESSIONS

kojā miri?	Where are you going?
kojā mirid?	Where are you going? (*polite*)
bā chi miri?	How are you going? (*lit.* with what are you going?)
bā tāksi miram	I'm going by taxi
vāllāh	Honestly, in truth
bāshe	OK (*spoken form of* **bāshad** = let it be, *the 3rd person singular of the subjunctive of* **budan**)
khodā nakone	God forbid!
bejomb	Be quick! hurry up! (*from* **jombidan**, to move); get a move on!

EXERCISES

A. Read aloud then translate:
1. havā sard-e, barf miād
2. mon<u>sh</u>i nāme minevise
3. har <u>ch</u>e zudtar miram
4. mi<u>kh</u>ām piāde beram mive be<u>kh</u>aram
5. Maryam az davā<u>kh</u>une barāye pesare<u>sh</u> davā mi<u>kh</u>are
6. mā barāye sobune nun o panir o <u>ch</u>āi mi<u>kh</u>orim
7. dustam natunest bā mā biād
8. fardā miram edāre
9. dar-o beband

B. Put into Persian:
1. Hassan goes to the office every day
2. She does not go there every day
3. It is raining
4. Are you English?
5. No, I am Iranian. I am not English
6. He wants to come to my house
7. I'll go tomorrow
8. Why did you (*plural*) come?
9. Where is he going?
10. Where are you going tomorrow?

C. Put the following into (a) the present tense; (b) the imperfect; (c) the subjunctive:
1. raftam
2. goftim
3. rundid
4. <u>kh</u>ordand
5. <u>sh</u>od

D. Give the imperative singular of the following:
1. to say
2. to hear
3. to eat
4. to run
5. to come

Lesson Five
(darse panjom)

Read aloud:

■ mosāfer be istgāhe otobus resid. az gishe chandtā bilit kharid chun dar Irān bilit o/rā dar otobus nemifrushand. mardom unhā ro/rā az gishe mikharand. otobus resid. hame savār shodand. dar ba'zi otobusā bilit o be rānande midand, dar ba'zihā ham be shāgerd-shofor. otobus rāh oftād. jā kam bud o chand nafar istādé budand. be istgāhe avval nazdik shodand. ye nafar sedā zad: āghā negah dār. otobus istād. rānande dar o bāz kard. chand nafar piāde shodand, dar basté shod o bāz otobus rāh oftad. rānande be sā'atash negāh kard – kami dir shodé bud.

Vocabulary:

avval	first	**mardom**	people
bāz (*adverb*)	again	**mosāfer**	passenger
ba'zi	some	**nafar**	person
basté	closed (*past participle*)	**negah dār**	stop!
		nazdik shod	approached
chand	some	**nemifrushand**	they don't sell
chandtā	several	**piāde shodand**	they got off
gishe	booth	**rānande**	driver
ham	also	**rāh oftād**	set off
hame	everyone, all	**savār shodand**	they got on
istgāh	stop	**sedā zad (zan)**	(he) called out
istgāhe otobus	bus stop	**sedā**	noise, voice
istād	stopped		

Note: **nemifrushand**: the verb is **forukhtan (forush)**; the **u** is elided in speech in tenses derived from the present stem.
Tenses formed from the past stem behave normally.

New verbs: **savār shodan (shav)**: to get on, to mount
rāh oftādan (oft): to set off, to start up

nazdik <u>sh</u>odan (<u>sh</u>av): to approach, to near
sedā zadan (zan): to call
negah dā<u>sh</u>tan (dār): to stop, to hold
piāde <u>sh</u>odan (<u>sh</u>av): to get off (*a bus etc.*)
bastan (band): to close
istādan (ist): to stand, to stop

USE OF THE PARTICLE RĀ

One of the characteristics of Persian is the use of the particle **rā** after the word or phrase that is the definite direct object of the verb.

Up to now we have used very simple basic sentence patterns which have tended to express states of being rather than actions:

dar baste ast	–	The door is closed
chāi hāzer-e	–	The tea is ready

but if we want to say 'he closed the door', then 'he' is the subject and 'the door' is the definite direct object – the specific thing to which the action is being done – in which case it will be followed by the particle **rā**.

rā is changed in speech to **ro** (following a word ending in a vowel sound) and **o** (following a consonant), though this is not necessarily very consistent, and you may notice such inconsistencies in this book.

dar o bast	–	He closed the door
chāi ro āvord	–	He brought the tea
bilit o <u>kh</u>arid	–	He bought the ticket
<u>gh</u>azā ro <u>kh</u>ord	–	He ate the food

If the direct object is a group of words, the **rā** comes after the group:

otobuse hotel o didam	–	I saw the hotel bus
moāvene vazir o did	–	He saw the deputy minister
sedāye radio ro <u>sh</u>enid	–	He heard the sound of the radio

Where a noun to which a pronominal suffix has been added

(**ketābam, ketābet**, etc.) is the direct object of the verb, then the **rā** is added after the suffix:

ketābam o gom kardam – I lost my book (**gom kardan**: to lose)
and if such a noun is qualified by an adjective, it follows the adjective:

ketābe sefidam o gom kardam – I lost my white book

Personal pronouns are definite and therefore take **rā** when they are the direct object of the verb:

> **man + rā = marā**
> **to + rā = torā** etc.

In speech these forms will be:

mano	**māro**
toro	**shomāro**
uno	**unāro**

khāharam mano zad – My sister hit me

A direct object can, however, be indefinite, in which case there will be no **rā**:

ye bilit kharid	–	He bought a ticket
ye ketāb āvord	–	She brought a book
ye chāi khord	–	He drank a cup of tea

the **ye** can also be left out:

bilit kharid	–	He bought a ticket
ketāb āvord	–	She brought a book
chāi khord	–	He drank some tea

Note: One does not, however, say **dar bast** to mean 'he closed a door'. In colloquial speech one always says **dar o bast**, as the door is considered to be a definite object in this case. The phrase **dar bast** is used adjectivally and is explained at the end of this lesson.

COMPOUND VERBS

Persian has relatively few simple verbs, therefore another feature of the language is the extensive use that is made of compound verbs. These consist of a few common verbs such as 'make', 'do', 'become', etc. coupled with a noun, adjective, adverb, verbal noun or preposition. In each case the verb is conjugated but the qualifying word remains unchanged throughout.

The verbs used most in compounds are:

kardan (kon) – to do, to make, *for transitive verbs*
shodan (shav) – to become, *for intransitive verbs*

> e.g.: **bāz** – open
> **kardan** – to do
> **bāz kardan** – to open

dar o bāz kard	– He opened the door
dar bāz shod	– The door opened
bachche man o khaste kard	– The child made me tired
khaste shodam	– I got tired

or, in the present tense:

dar o bāz mikone	– He opens the door
dar bāz mishe	– The door opens
bachche man o khaste mikone	– The child makes me tired
khaste misham	– I get tired

Compound verbs are used as if they were a single verb, i.e. they generally come at the end of the sentence and the separate parts are placed together.

They are conjugated normally, the only difference being in the imperative, where the verb does not take the prefix **be-** so that whereas the imperative of **kardan** used on its own will be **bekon**, in a compound it is **kon**:

> **dar o bāz kon** – Open the door

Look again at this phrase from the reading passage at the beginning of this lesson:

āghā negah dār (the verb is **negah dāshtan**)

and note that when **dāshtan** is being used as a compound verb, its imperative is formed regularly.

The following are some more verbs generally used to form compounds:

dāshtan (dār)	to have, to possess
dādan (deh/dah)	to give
gereftan (gir)	to take, to get
zadan (zan)	to hit, to strike
khordan (khor)	to eat
āmadan (ā)	to come
āvardan (ār) (*coll.* āvordan)	to bring

Some examples of compound verbs are:

(*a*) with adjectives:

boland – long, tall, high
boland kardan – to lift (*also* to lengthen)
boland shodan – to get up

khub – good
khub shodan – to get well, to get better

Note that in general the English 'to get . . .' will be rendered by a compound verb with **shodan**.

kutā – short
kutā kardan – to shorten

dorost – correct, right, proper
dorost kardan – to make, fix, mend (*a much-used compound verb*)

sandali ro boland kard	–	He picked up the chair
az jāsh/jāyash boland shod	–	She got up from her place
mariz khub shod	–	The patient got better
emtahānam khub shod	–	I did well in my exam
dāmanesh o kutā kard	–	She shortened her skirt
ghazā ro dorost kard	–	She got the meal
takhtekhāb o dorost kard	–	She made the bed
māshinesh o dorost kard	–	He fixed the car

(*b*) with nouns:

gush	–	ear
gush kardan	–	to listen
gush dādan	–	to listen

hammām (*coll.* hamum)	–	bath
hamun kardan	–	to have a bath
du<u>sh</u>	–	shower
du<u>sh</u> gereftan	–	to have a shower
farār kardan	–	to escape (*see also* dar raftan *in section (c)*)
dast	–	hand
dast dādan	–	to shake hands
zamin	–	ground, land, earth (*not* soil *which is* <u>kh</u>āk)
zamin <u>kh</u>ordan	–	to fall down (*lit.* to eat the ground)
be a<u>kh</u>bār gu<u>sh</u> kard	–	She listened to the news
bā duste<u>sh</u> dast dād	–	He shook hands with his friend
bachche zamin <u>kh</u>ord	–	The child fell down

(c) with prepositions:

bar (on, up, off)

bar dā<u>sh</u>tan	–	to remove, to pick up, to take
bar ga<u>sh</u>tan	–	to return, to come/go back
ketāb o bar dā<u>sh</u>t	–	She picked up the book
fardā bar migardam	–	I'll come back tomorrow

dar (in)

dar āvordan	–	to take off, to take out
dar raftan	–	to escape (*more colloquial than* farār kardan), to get away, to go off (*guns etc.*), to snap (*elastic*), to ladder (*stockings*)
dar kardan	–	to let off (*a gun etc.*)
lebāse<u>sh</u> o dar āvord	–	She took off her dress
gorbe dar raft	–	The cat got away
jurābam dar raft	–	I laddered my stocking (*lit:* my stocking ran away)

(*d*) with prepositional phrases:

az bêın raftan	–	to cease to exist
az dast dādan	–	to lose (*a person through death, a contract, a job, etc.*; to lose things *is another compound* **gom kardan**; to get lost *is* **gom shodan**)

COMPOUND TENSES

The compound tenses of single verbs are the perfect, the pluperfect, the future, the past subjunctive and the passive. They are formed with the use of the verbs **budan (bāsh)** 'to be', **khāstan (khāh)** 'to want' and **shodan (shav)** 'to become', which therefore act as auxiliary verbs.

1. The Perfect

This is formed from the past participle with the addition of the short forms of the verb 'to be':

-am	-im
-i	-id
ast	-and

The past participle consists of the past stem with an accented **e** sound (transcribed **é**) on the end: **raftan – raft – rafté**.

The forms of the perfect tense are:

rafté-am (I have gone)	**rafté-im** (we have gone)
rafté-i	**rafté-id**
rafté ast	**rafté-and**
rāndé-am (I have driven)	**rāndé-im** (we have driven)
rāndé-i	**rāndé-id**
rāndé ast	**rāndé-and**

The perfect tense is generally contracted in speech so that it sounds very much like the simple past, except that the stress is now on the last syllable and not the first:

raft-am	raft-im
raft-i	raft-id
raft ast	raft-and
rānd-am	rānd-im
rānd-id	rānd-id
rānd ast	rānd-and

In the third person singular, it is also quite common in speech to use the past participle on its own when in fact the perfect is meant:-

otobus rafté	–	The bus has gone

The negative prefix is **na-**, which then carries the stress:

otobus narafté	–	The bus hasn't gone

The perfect tense is quite common in colloquial Persian. It usually refers to actions which have recently been completed or which started in the past but which haven't yet been completed:

ketāb o āvordé-am	–	I have brought the book
ruznāme rā khundé-am	–	I have read the newspaper
tāksi āmadé ast	–	The taxi has come
Maryam khābidé ast	–	Mariam is sleeping

2. The Pluperfect

The pluperfect is formed from the past participle, which does not change, and the simple past of **budan**:

rafté budam (I had gone)	rafté budim (we had gone)
rafté budi	rafté budid
rafté bud	rafté budand

The use of the pluperfect in Persian is much the same as in English, except that it is also used as a descriptive tense in the past: **istādé bud** = was standing, stood.

3. The Future

The future tense is formed by using the present tense of the verb **khāstan (khāh)** 'to want', minus the usual verbal prefix **mi-**, followed by the past stem of the verb:

khāham raft (I will go)	**khāhim raft** (we will go)
khāhi raft	**khāhid raft**
khāhad raft	**khāhand raft**

The future proper is used in formal speech (radio and television news or announcements, for example) but in colloquial speech the present tense is used instead, as already indicated in Lesson Four.

Note that whenever **khāstan** is used in its own sense and not as an auxiliary, it behaves quite normally in the present tense:

chāi mikham	–	I want some tea
mikham beram khune	–	I want to go home

4. The Past Subjunctive

The past subjunctive is formed by using the past participle followed by the present subjunctive of the verb **budan**:

rafté bāsham (I may have gone)	**rafté bāshim**
rafté bāshi	**rafté bāshid**
rafté bāshe/bāshad	**rafté bāshand**

The past subjunctive is used:
(*a*) after **bāyad** and **shāyad** when they refer to the past:

bāyad rafté bāshe	–	He must have gone
shāyad in o didé bāshi	–	Perhaps you've seen this

(*b*) to express doubt about something in the past:

mitarsam gom shodé bāshe	–	I'm afraid it may have got lost

(*c*) as the present subjunctive of **dāshtan** (see Lesson Four).

5. The Passive

The passive is formed by using the past participle followed by the appropriate tense of the verb **shodan** (**shav**) 'to become':

e.g. from **koshtan** (**kosh**) to kill:

koshté shod	he/she/it was killed
koshté misham	I shall be killed etc.

Use of the passive is very restricted in Persian and it is not used if the active can be used instead.

■ PHRASES AND EXPRESSIONS

dar bast

Exclusive – *in relation to the hire of cars, taxis or even buses; if they are* **dar bast** *it means no one other than the person hiring them (or members of their party) will use them. The phrase is relevant because ordinary taxis, for example, are by no means* **dar bast**. *They pick up several passengers as they go, depending on whether their destinations fit the route the taxi happens to be taking.*

befarmāid

lit. the imperative of **farmudan** 'to command'. *This is a very common word, used*
1. *when giving or showing someone something to mean* 'here you are'
2. *in the sense of* 'after you'
3. *in the sense of* 'come in'
4. *by people serving the public in shops, offices etc. to mean* 'what can I do for you?'

khāhesh mikonam

Please, *when asking someone to do something* (from **khāhesh kardan** 'to request politely', 'to ask a favour'). **khāhesh mikonam** *can be used at the beginning or at the end of a sentence or phrase e.g.* **khāhesh mikonam dar rā bāz konid** = please open the door.

begu bebinam

Tell me, . . . *e.g.* **begu bebinam emruz kojā mirim** tell me, where are we going today

begid bebinam   *polite form of* **begu bebinam**

■ *Some useful commands:*

bar gard/bar gardid	–	Come back! (*familiar/polite*)
boro/berid	–	Go! (*familiar/polite*)
bāz kon/bāz konid	–	Open!
dar o beband	–	Shut the door!
dar o bebandid	–	Shut the door! (*polite*)
beshin/beshinid	–	Sit down! (*familiar/polite*)
boland sho	–	Get up!, Stand up!
boland shid	–	Get up!, Stand up! (*polite*)

EXERCISES

A. Read aloud and translate:

1. rānande dar o bāz kard
2. pesaram dar o bast
3. ketāb o āvord
4. bilite otobus o az gishe kharid
5. pesare sheîtun kheîli zamin mikhore
6. be hotel raftam o hamum kardam
7. havā kheîli sard shodé vo har ruz bārun miād
8. lebāsam o dar āvordam
9. dar o bāz kon. nazdike āb naro. panjere ro beband
10. dir residam o otobus rafté bud

B. Put into Persian:

1. He closed the door; she brought the tea; they ate the food
2. He bought a newspaper; she drank a cup of tea; we had some food (*i.e. we ate*)
3. They saw the hotel bus
4. We saw the deputy minister
5. My friend opened the door. He said: "Come in"
6. Someone called out: 'Stop'
7. Do not open the door
8. Please close the window
9. The bus has gone
10. Has the taxi come?

SUMMARY OF VERB ENDINGS

PRESENT:	mi- + *present stem* +	-am	-im
		-i	-id
		-ad	-and
IMPERFECT:	mi- + *past stem* +	-am	-im
		-i	-id
		-	-and
PRETERITE:	*past stem* +	-am	-im
		-i	-id
		-	-and
PERFECT:	*past participle* +	-am	-im
		-i	-id
		ast	-and
PLUPERFECT:	*past participle* +	budam	budim
		budi	budid
		bud	budand

FUTURE PROPER:	k͟hāham	k͟hāhim + *past stem*
	k͟hāhi	k͟hāhid
	k͟hāhad	k͟hāhand

PRESENT SUBJUNCTIVE:	be + *present stem* +	-am	-im
		-i	-id
		-ad	-and
PAST SUBJUNCTIVE:	*past participle* +	bāsham	bāshim
		bāshi	bāshid
		bāshad	bāshand

IMPERATIVE: be/bo + *present stem*

NEGATIVE IMPERATIVE: na- + *present stem*

The -ad of the 3rd person singular present and subjunctive is shortened to -e in speech.

Lesson Six
(darse <u>shish</u>om)

Read aloud:

■ pāyeta<u>kh</u>te Irān Tehrān-e. Tehrān <u>sh</u>ahre bozorgi-e va ta<u>gh</u>riban noh meliun nafar jam'iyat dāre. bi<u>sh</u>tare unhā dar <u>gh</u>esmathāye jonubiye <u>sh</u>ahr zendegi mikonand. bi<u>sh</u>tare edārehā dar <u>gh</u>esmathāye markaziye <u>sh</u>ahr-and. esme <u>gh</u>esmate <u>sh</u>omāliye <u>sh</u>āhr <u>Sh</u>emrun-e. <u>Sh</u>emrun dar dāmaneye kuhāye Alborz-e. bi<u>sh</u>tare <u>kh</u>unehāye bozorge Tehrān dar <u>Sh</u>emrun-and <u>ch</u>un havāye unjā dar tābestun <u>kh</u>onaktar az <u>gh</u>esmathāye digeye <u>sh</u>ahr-e. asrhāye tābestun mardom ba'd az kāre<u>sh</u>un barāye garde<u>sh</u> o tafrih o estefade az havāye behtar be mêɪdānhā vo pārkhāye <u>Sh</u>emrun mirand o garde<u>sh</u> mikonand. bi<u>sh</u>tar bā mā<u>sh</u>ine <u>sh</u>akhsi mirand, gar <u>ch</u>e bā otobus o tāksi ham mi<u>sh</u>e raft. havāye Tehrān dar tābestun <u>kh</u>êɪli garm va dar zemestun <u>kh</u>êɪli sard-e. bārun kamtar az Engelestān mibāre. dar zemestān gāhi barf ziād mibāre. dar jonube Tehrān, dar <u>sh</u>ahre <u>gh</u>adimiye Rey, pālāye<u>sh</u>gāhe Tehrān va <u>ch</u>and karkhuneye dige <u>gh</u>arār gerefté. dāne<u>sh</u>gāhe Tehrān dar vasate <u>sh</u>ahr-e. har hafte mardom barāye namāze jom'e be unjā mirand.

Vocabulary:

asrhā	evenings	**gharār gerefté**	is situated
bārun	rain	**ghesmathā**	parts, sections
bāridan (bār)	to fall (*of rain, snow etc*)	**jam'iyat**	population
		jonub	south
dāne<u>sh</u>gāh	university	**kār**	work
dāmane	foothills	**kārkhune**	factory
dige/digar	other	**kuhā**	mountains
Engelestān	England	**khonak**	cool
esm	name	**markazi**	central
gāhi	sometimes	**meliun**	million
garde<u>sh</u>	outing	**mibāre**	it falls
gar <u>ch</u>e	although	**nafar**	persons
<u>gh</u>adimi	old	**namāz**	prayers

noh	nine	**tafrih**	recreation
pālāyeshgāh	refinery	**taghriban**	approximately
pāyetakht	capital	**vasat(e)**	middle (of)
shakhsi	personal	**zemestun/ān**	winter
shomāli	northern	**zendegi**	they live
tābestun/ān	summer	**mikonand**	

Notes: **mishe raft**: one can go; in addition to 'become', the verb **shodan** also has the meaning of 'it is possible', and is used in this kind of impersonal construction.

namāz: the name for the prayers which every practising Moslem must say five times a day. It is one of the most important of the practical religious duties – others are fasting, almsgiving and pilgrimage. On Fridays it is customary for the noon prayers to be said in congregation in the mosque. The word for ordinary prayer is **do'ā**, the verb is **do'ā kardan (kon)**

ADVERBS AND ADVERBIAL EXPRESSIONS

Adverbs or adverbial expressions of time usually come before those of manner and place. If a sentence contains all three, then the order will be: time, manner, place e.g.:

har ruz bā tāksi be edāre miram – I go to the office by taxi every day

1. Most adjectives are used as adverbs in Persian without any change:

dir āmad	–	He came late
zud raft	–	She went/left early
khub mikhune	–	She reads well
bad mirune	–	He drives badly
rāst boro	–	Go straight on
dorost beshin/beneshin	–	Sit properly

2. Many nouns of time and place are also used adverbially:

sob dars mikhune	–	He studies in the morning
shab kār mikone	–	He works at night
ruz mikhābe	–	He sleeps during the day
asr bārun āmad	–	It rained in the evening
zohr namāz mikhune	–	She says her prayers at noon
ghorub āb pāchi mikone	–	He does the watering at dusk
sahar pā mishe	–	She gets up at dawn (*pā shodan*)
ketāb o bezar injā	–	Put the book here
unjā naraftam	–	I didn't go there
az pelle bālā raft	–	He went up the steps

It is also very common in speech for these nouns to be put in the plural when being used adverbially:

sobā ruznāme mikhune	–	He reads the paper in the mornings
shabā ketāb mikhunam	–	I read books at night
asrā kelās mire	–	He goes to classes in the evenings

3. Other adverbs of time and manner are:

(a) *Time*:

emruz	–	today
diruz	–	yesterday
pariruz	–	the day before yesterday
dishab	–	last night
fardā	–	tomorrow
pasfardā	–	the day after tomorrow
hamishe	–	always
hālā	–	now
māhyune	–	monthly
emsāl	–	this year
pārsāl	–	last year
hanuz	–	still
hanuz . . . na-	–	not yet
hichvaght	–	never
har gez	–	never
al'ān	–	right now; just

tā hālā	–	up to now; yet
bārhā	–	often, many times
gāhi	–	sometimes
yek dafe	–	suddenly (*lit.* one time, one)
emruz miram khuneye dustam	–	I'm going to my friend's house today
diruz maghāze baste bud	–	The shop was shut yesterday
pariruz raftam bāzār	–	I went to the bazaar the day before yesterday
dishab dir khābidam	–	I went to bed late last night
fardā zud boland misham	–	I'll get up early tomorrow
pasfardā miram salmuni	–	I'll go to the hairdressers the day after tomorrow
hamishe ketāb mikhune	–	He's always reading
hamishe mire masjed	–	He always goes to the mosque
hālā vaght nadāram	–	I've no time now
majaleye Dāneshmand māhyune dar miād	–	'Daneshmand' appears monthly
emsāl bārun ziād umad	–	It rained a lot this year
pārsāl mive farāvun bud	–	Fruit was plentiful last year
hanuz barf miād	–	It's still snowing
dustam hanuz nayāmade	–	My friend hasn't come yet
dustet hanuz nayāmade?	–	Hasn't your friend come yet?
hichvaght havāpêimā savār nashodé bud	–	He had never been on a plane
har gez torā farāmush nemikonam	–	I'll never forget you
al'ān miām	–	I'm coming right now
al'ān telefon kard	–	She just telephoned
tā hālā khub kār kardé	–	It has worked well up to now
tā hālā telefon nakardé	–	She hasn't telephoned yet
bārhā be manzele man āmadé bud	–	He had come to my house many times
gāhi u rā mibinam	–	I see him sometimes
yek dafe tārik shod	–	It suddenly went dark

Note: 'often' is frequently rendered in colloquial speech by **khêli** ('very') which is like the English use of 'a lot':

khêli be manzele man āmadé – He has come to my house a lot

(b) Manner:

āheste	–	slowly
yavā<u>sh</u>	–	slowly
tond	–	fast
albatte	–	certainly
tanhā	–	alone
bā ham	–	together
intowr	–	thus, in this way, like this
untowr	–	like that
<u>ch</u>etowr	–	how

tond naro	–	Don't go fast
yavā<u>sh</u> boro	–	Go slowly
āheste berānid	–	Drive slowly
tanhā birun naro	–	Don't go out alone
biā bā ham berim garde<u>sh</u>	–	Let's go somewhere together
untowr nist	–	It's not like that

4. Some adverbs are derived from Arabic and usually end in **-an**:

a<u>gh</u>allan	–	at least
<u>gh</u>ablan	–	formerly
mova<u>gh</u>attan	–	temporarily
ta<u>gh</u>riban	–	approximately
fe'lan	–	for the time being, for the moment
masalan	–	for example
aslan	–	at all
bela<u>kh</u>are	–	at last, finally

a<u>gh</u>allan sadtā mā<u>sh</u>in tuye saf bud	–	There were at least a hundred cars in the queue
injā <u>gh</u>ablan madrese bud	–	This [place] was formerly a school
edāreye bar<u>gh</u> fyuzemun o mova<u>gh</u>attan dorost kard	–	The electricity board temporarily mended our fuse
ta<u>gh</u>riban panjāh nafar āmadé budan	–	There were about fifty people there
fe'lan nemitunam biām	–	I can't come for the moment

PREPOSITIONS

There are two groups of prepositions used in Persian, those without the *ezāfe* and those which are connected to the noun by means of the *ezāfe*. Some of these have already been used in the reading passages at the beginning of the lessons.

Prepositions always come before the noun to which they refer.

Prepositions without the *ezāfe* are:

az	–	from
bā	–	with
barāye	–	for
be	–	to
bi	–	without
tā	–	up to, to, as far as
joz	–	except
dar	–	in
bar	–	on (*in compounds*)

az

az has a wide variety of meanings:

In Lesson Two we saw its use to express 'than' in comparisons:

māshine man az māshine to bozorgtare	– My car is bigger than yours

The most common meaning of **az**, however, is 'from':

e.g.:

az dustam nāme dāshtam	– I had a letter from my friend
az hotel telefon mikonam	– I am phoning from the hotel
mive ro az bāzār kharidam	– I bought the fruit from the bazaar
az Tehrān tā Tabriz sheshsad kilometr-e	– It is six hundred kilometres from Tehran to Tabriz
kilide otāgh o az man gereft	– He took the key of the room from me

az kojā āmadé-id?	– Where have you come from?

az can also mean 'through/in':

az dar āmad	– He/she came through/in the door
az dar vāred shod	– He/she entered through the door

or 'of':

kami az in bokhor – Have some of this

bā: with

dastam o bā āb o sābun shostam	– I washed my hands with soap and water
Maryam bā khāharesh raft madrese	– Mariam went to school with her sister
bā dustam raftam mehmuni	– I went to a party with my friend
bā ham ghazā khordim	– We ate together
bā mo'āvene vazir sohbat kardam (**sohbat kardan** – to speak)	– I spoke to the deputy minister

barāye: for

loftan barāye man yek chāi biārid	– Please bring me a cup of tea
kār kardan barāye man sakht-e	– Work is difficult for me
barāye chi āmadi?	– What did you come for?

be: to

be man telefon kon	– Telephone me
ketāb o behesh dād	– He gave him the book
be Irān umad	– He/she came to Iran (**umad/āmad**: both forms are used)
behem negā kard/be man negā kard	– He/she looked at me

Note that in colloquial speech the forms **be man**, **be to**, **be u** etc., become shortened as follows:

behem	to me	**behemān**	to us
behet	to you	**behetān**	to you
behe<u>sh</u>	to him/her	**behe<u>sh</u>ān**	to them

bi: without

bi is most often used almost as a prefix, rather on the lines of the English suffix -*less*:

    tavajjoh – care
    bi tavajjoh – careless

    kār – work
    bikār – without work, *also*, having nothing to do

    adab, tarbiat – politeness
    bi adab – rude
    bi tarbiat – rude

    man <u>gh</u>azāye bi namak mi<u>kh</u>oram – I eat unsalted food

tā: as far as, up to, to
    az manzel tā edāre piāde raft – He walked from the house to the office

joz: except

    joz fardā har ruz āzād hastam – I am free every day except tomorrow

dar: in
    mo'allem dar kelās bud – The teacher was in the classroom

dar is more generally formal except in certain expressions (see phrases and expressions at the end of this lesson). In colloquial speech **tu** (or **tuye**, with the *ezāfe*) is much more widely used to render 'in':

biã tu	– Come in
befarmãid tu	– Come in (*more polite*)
nãme ro tuye kifam gozãshtam	– I put the letter in my bag

Prepositions which take the *ezãfe* and which are derived from adverbs and nouns are:

bedune: without	– bedune hejãb birun naro
birune: outside	– birune shahr kãrkhune ziãd-e
tuye: inside, in	– tuye otãgh khêıli garm bud
pãine: below	– pãine pellehã istãdé bud
balãye: above; up	– pesar balãye derakht bud
dombãle: behind, after	– dombãle man biã
poshte: behind	– poshte miz neshasté bud
jeloye: in front of	– jeloye man bãzesh kard
pishe: with	- tamãme ruz pishe man bud
dame: on the edge of, at	– dame dar montazeret misham
zire: under	– kafshã ro zire takht gozãshtam
ruye: on	– zarfe mive ruye miz-e
nazdike: near	– Karaj nazdike Tehrãn-e
pahluye: beside	– dustam pahluye man neshasté bud
kenãre: beside	– kenãre rudkhune ghadam zadim

Vocabulary:
hejãb: prescribed Islamic covering for women
pellehã: steps
montazer shodan: to wait for
zarf: dish
rudkhune: river
ghadam zadan: to stroll

■ PHRASES AND EXPRESSIONS

magar, *coll.* **mage**	*preposition, literally meaning* except
mage nagoftam naro	Didn't I tell you not to go?
mage nayumad	Didn't he come?
mage nabud	Wasn't it/he/she there?, wasn't it so?
mage kāret tamum na<u>sh</u>od	Wasn't your work finished?
dar havāye āzād	In the open air
dar ham bar ham	Muddled, all mixed up together
az bas ke	So much so that
az sob tā <u>sh</u>ab	From morn till night
kame kam	At the very least
dar har hāl	In any case, at all events
be har hāl	In any case, anyway
har towr <u>sh</u>odé	Come what may
aze<u>sh</u> badam umad	I took a dislike to him
cherā	Yes (*in answer to a negative question*)

EXERCISES

A. Read aloud and translate

1. man o dustam pariruz raftim sinemā
2. fardā biā bā ham berim <u>kh</u>arid
3. di<u>sh</u>ab cherā unghadr dir āmadi?
4. ta<u>gh</u>riban bist da<u>gh</u>ighe sabr kardam ammā otobus nayāmad
5. pedaram hanuz az mosāferat bar naga<u>sh</u>té
6. cherā bā ham naraftid
7. edāram nazdike bāzār-e
8. sāle dige miram dāne<u>sh</u>gāh
9. pārsāl bā mā<u>sh</u>in be Torkiyye raftim
10. otobuse <u>sh</u>ahr sob o asr az jeloye <u>kh</u>uneye mā rad mi<u>sh</u>e
11. ā<u>gh</u>ā, kaf<u>sh</u>e mano nadidid?
    cherā – zire ta<u>kh</u>tetun-e
12. begu bebinam, joz to kese digei ham umadé bud?

B. Put into Persian:
1. The glass was on the table
2. The child went slowly up the stairs
3. I finished my work yesterday
4. We went to Paris last year
5. My friend drives well
6. My daughter came home late
7. The train travels very fast (*use* raftan)
8. Put your bag here
9. How did you come?
10. They flew to London last year (*say* 'went by plane')

C. Fill in the blanks:
1. ———————— man biā
2. nāme ro ———————— vazir bede
3. ketāb o ———————— unjā nakharidam
4. pedaram ———————— man kafsh kharid
5. ———————— kojā āmadi?
6. māshin o ———————— gārāzh gozāshtam
7. ———————— dustam telefon kardam

Lesson Seven (darse haftom)

Read aloud:

■ Irān keshvare bozorgiy-e. hodude yek melyun o sheshsad o si hezār kilometre morabba' masāhat dāre vo bishtar az panjāh melyun nafar ham jam'iyyat. taghriban yek panjome unhā dar Tehrān zendegi mikonand. shahrhāye bozorge dige Mashhad, Tabriz, Esfahān, Shirāz o Ahvāz hastand. inhā har kudum az hamdige khêili dur-and. masalan az Tehrān tā Tabriz yā Esfahān sheshsad kilometr rāh-e. dar shomāle Irān daryāye Khezer gharār gerefté va dar jonub Khalije Fārs. chand reshte kuhe bozorg ham az shargh be gharb va az shomāl be jonub keshidé shodé. meghdāre ziādi az ghesmathāye markazi va sharghiye Irān kavir-e vā zendegi dar unjā khêili sakht-e. faghat mantagheye sāheliye Daryāye Khezer bārandegiye kāfi dāre va havāye martube unjā barāye keshte berenj o chāi monāseb-e.

Vocabulary:

bārandegi	rainfall	**mantaghe**	region
berenj	rice	**markazi**	central
daryā	sea	**martub**	moist
daryāye Khezer	the Caspian sea	**masāhat**	area (*in terms of quantity*)
dur	far	**masalan**	for example
faghat	only	**melyun**	million
gharb	west	**metr**	metre
gharār gerefté	is situated	**monāseb**	suitable
ghesmat	section	**morabbā'**	square (*area*)
hamdige	each other	**panjāh**	fifty
hezār	thousand	**rāh**	way, road
hodude	about	**reshte**	range
jam'iyyat	population	**sāheli**	coastal
jonub	south	**shargh**	east
kāfi	sufficient	**sheshsad**	six hundred
kavir	salt desert	**shomāl**	north
keshvar	country	**yek panjom**	a fifth
keshidé shodé	are stretched	**zendegi**	life
kesht	cultivation	**zendegi mikonand**	they live
kilometr	kilometer		
khalij	gulf		
khalije Fārs	the Persian Gulf		

NUMBERS

Unlike the script which is written from right to left, numbers are written from left to right as in English (See Appendix).

1. *The cardinal numbers are:*

0	sefr	3	se
1	yek	4	chār/chahār
2	do	5	panj

6	shish	30	si
7	haft	40	chel/chehel
8	hasht	50	panjāh
9	noh	60	shast
10	dah	70	haftād
11	yāzdah	80	hashtād
12	davāzdah	90	navad
13	sizdah	100	sad (*a hundred*)
14	chārdah/chahārdah		yeksad (*one hundred*)
15	punzdah	101	sad-o-yek
16	shunzdah	102	sad-o-do
17	hivdah	121	sad-o-bist-o-yek *etc*
18	hizhdah	200	divist
19	nuzdah	300	sisad
20	bist	400	chārsad/chahārsad
21	bist-o-yek	500	punsad *etc.*
22	bist-o-do	1000	hezār
23	bist-o-se	1,000,000	melyun
24	bist-o-chār *etc.*		

Note: The final **h** after the vowel (as in **noh, dah, yāzdah**, etc. is hardly pronounced at all, but it has been written in to avoid confusion when forming the ordinal numbers where it *is* pronounced (see paragraph 2).

(*a*) When speaking of things, the word **dune/dāne** (*lit.* grain, seed) is often used as an itemiser: *ye dune ketāb kharidam.* For people, **nafar** (*person*) is used: **ye nafar āmad.**

(*b*) When speaking of numbers of things (i.e. more than one), the suffix **-tā** is added to the cardinal number and the noun remains in the singular:

Hasan behesh dotā ketāb dad – Hasan gave him two books
setā chamedun dāram – I have three suitcases

BUT for people and time (hours, days, months, years etc) the number stands alone:

man do ruz unjā mundam – I stayed there for two days
emshab panj nafar – I have five guests this
mehmun dāram evening

baradaram se sal dar engelestan bud	– My brother was in England for three years
Hasan panj sa'at dar khuneye Akbar mund	– Hassan stayed at Akbar's house for five hours

(c) __chandta__/__chand__ – how many?/how much?

In the same way, when asking 'how many?' (things), the question is asked using __chandta__:

> __chandta__ ketab dari? – panjta
> Maryam __chandta__ ketab dare? – __shishta__
> __chandta__ nun kharidi? – seta

For people and time, the same distinction applies as in (b) above:

> __chand__ nafar umadand? – __shish__ nafar
> __chand__ sa'at rah darim? – haft sa'at
> __chand__ ruz kar dari? – se ruz
> __chand__ sal unja budi? – panj sal

(d) The expression 'how old are you?' which would, strictly speaking, be __chand__ sal dari/darid? – how many years do you have? – is always rendered colloquially as:

> __chand__ salet-e (i.e. _chand salat ast_)
> __chand__ saletun-e (_chand saletan ast_)

> pesaretun __chand__ salesh-e? – How old is your son?

(e) __chand__ is also used for 'how much?' when asking the price of something:

in ketab __chand-e?__	–	How much is this book?
bilite otobus __chand-e?__	–	How much are bus tickets?
khiar yeki __chand-e?__	–	How much are cucumbers each? (_for things sold singly_)
gusht kiloi __chand-e?__	–	How much is meat per kilo?

One can also just name the object, followed by __chand-e:__

taksi __chand-e?__	–	How much are taxis? (i.e. _the fare_)
portaghal __chand-e?__	–	How much are oranges?
daftar __chand-e?__	–	How much are exercise books?

in <u>ch</u>and-e?   –   How much is this?

(f) The same expression is used for asking the time:

sā'at <u>ch</u>and-e?   –   What is the time? (See also Lesson 8)

but remember, <u>ch</u>and sā'at? – how many hours? in (c) above.

2. The ordinal numbers are:

avval – first. This is an Arabic word and is always used to mean 'first', not yekom as would be expected, e.g. ruze avval – the first day. yekom is used in compound numbers, such as 'twenty-first' – bist-o-yekom.

dovvom (coll. = doyyom) – second
sevvom (coll. = seyyom) – third
chahārom (coll. chārom) – fourth
panjom etc., the remaining ordinal numbers being formed by the addition of -om to the cardinal number. Where the cardinal number is a group of numbers e.g. bist-o-yek, the last number takes the -om: bist-o-yekom, sad-o-bist-o-dovvom etc.

3. Fractions

Mathematical fractions are expressed by the use of the cardinal number followed by the ordinal:

yek dovvom	–	$\frac{1}{2}$
yek sevvom	–	$\frac{1}{3}$
yek <u>ch</u>ārom	–	$\frac{1}{4}$
se panjom	–	$\frac{3}{5}$
haft davāzdahom	–	$\frac{7}{12}$

The Arabic forms nesf (and its Persian equivalent nim), sols and rob' are also commonly used for 'half', 'third' and 'quarter' respectively.

(a) nesf and nim: both mean 'half', but are not necessarily interchangeable:

    (i) nesf: when used as a noun, nesf always takes the ezāfe:

nesfe <u>sh</u>ab   –   the middle of the night, midnight

nesfe ruz	–	half-day (*but not* midday, *which is* **zohr**)
nesfe pule<u>sh</u>	–	half of his money
nesfe ketāb	–	half the book
nesfe kāram o tamum kardam	–	I finished half of my work

(ii) **nim**: is usually used in expressions of quantity or measurement:

nim kilo	–	half a kilo
nim sā'at	–	half an hour
nim nomre	–	half a mark (*or* shoe size)
nim metr	–	half a metre

also 'one and a half', 'two and a half', etc. always use **nim**:

yek o nim	–	one and a half
bist o panj o nim	–	twenty-five and a half

(*b*) **sols**, 'a third', is much less commonly used in colloquial speech where it is preferable to say **yek sevvom** or **ye sevvom**. The word **sols** is most commonly found in schools where it refers to a third of the academic year – the equivalent of the English term. Children go to school for nine months consecutively (apart from 13 days' holiday for the new year), and exams are held at the end of each **sols**, with the aggregate of the three sets of marks deciding a pass or a fail at the end of the year.

(*c*) **rob'**, 'a quarter', is most commonly used in telling the time (Lesson Eight) or in expressions to do with time:

panj o rob'	–	a quarter past five
rob' sā'at	–	a quarter of an hour
ye rob' dige	–	in a quarter of an hour, another quarter of an hour

'a quarter of a kilo' will usually be referred to as **divist o panjā geram** (250 grammes) and 'a quarter of a meter' when buying things by length, such as material, wire, ribbon etc., will be referred to as **bist o panj sānt**.

4. *To say once, twice, etc.*, the cardinal numbers are used, followed by **dafe/daf'e**, **bār** or **martabe** ('times'):

ye/yek dafe	ye bār	ye martabe	–	once, one time
do dafe	do bār	do martabe	–	twice
se dafe	se bār	se martabe	–	three times

> *Note*: **ye/yek dafe** and **ye martabe** are also used as expressions to mean 'suddenly' (i.e. 'all at once'); **do martabe** is also used in the sense 'again'

'twice as much', 'twice as many', are expressed by the cardinal number followed by the word **barābar** ('equal'). In colloquial speech this construction is also used to express 'double', 'triple', *etc.*:

do barābar	–	double
se barābar	–	triple
panj barābar	–	five times
sad barābar	–	a hundred times

5. *Weights & Measures*
The metric system is used:

metr – meter
sāntimetr – centimeter (*often shortened to* **sānt**)
milimetr
kilometr

metre morabba'	–	square meter
hektār	–	hectare

geram	–	gramme
kilogeram/kilo	–	kilo

e.g.	**diruz do metr pārche kharidam**	– I bought two metres of fabric yesterday
	bi zahmat se metr o bist o panj sānt az in bedid	– Please give me three metres and twenty-five centimetres of this
	emruz se kilo gusht kharidam	– I bought three kilos of meat today
	az Tehrān tā Karaj chehel kilometr-e	– It is forty kilometres from Tehran to Karaj

chand geram kare lāzem dāram — I need a few grammes of butter

Note the difference in the use of the singular and plural in Persian and English – the words **kilo, metr** etc. are not put into the plural.

■ PHRASES AND EXPRESSIONS

Here are some more useful numerical phrases:

dollā	Double; two-fold (**lā** *means* layer, fold)
sellā	Triple; three-fold
chārlā	Quadruple
yeki yeki	One by one
ye-ruz-dar-miun	On alternate days, every other day (*lit.* one day in the middle)
se-ruz-dar-miun	Every three days
se-ruz-be-se-ruz	Every three days
yeki dotā	One or two
se chārtā ketāb	Three or four books
yeki do nafar	One or two people
do se sā'at	Two or three hours
māh be māh	Each month
ye joft jurāb	A pair of socks
ye livān āb	A glass of water

EXERCISES

A. Read aloud and translate:

1. sad o siyo panj nafar dar edāreye mā kār mikonand
2. mādaram dotā pirhane sefid kharid
3. chandtā bachche dārid?
4. barāye man se kilo gusht bekhar
5. chandtā khāhar barādar dāre?
6. chand nafar tuye otobus budand?
7. yek sevvome pulesho beman dād
8. panj shish metr pārche lāzem dāram
9. ghêimate khune bist dar sad bālā rafté
10. az kojā mitunam ye joft kafshe khub bekharam?

B. Put into Persian:
1. How old are you? (*Polite and familiar*)
2. I'm forty-five
3. My son is four years old
4. He ate half of the loaf (= *bread*)
5. There are two big mountain ranges in Iran
6. I telephoned them three times
7. He has been to my office twice
8. I saw the minister once
9. How much are these oranges per kilo?
10. How many people were there in the room?

Lesson Eight (darse ha<u>sh</u>tom)

Read aloud:

ÊIDE NOW RUZ

avvale Farvardin ruze avvale sāl va êide now ruz-e. now ruz <u>sh</u>oru'e sāle jadid va êide <u>gh</u>adimiye Irān-e. har sāl barāye êid edārehā se tā panj ruz ta'tiland va madresehā sizdah ruz. dar sā'ate tahvile sāle now <u>kh</u>ānevādehā lebāse now mipu<u>sh</u>and, sare sofreye haftsin dowre ham jam mi<u>sh</u>and o montazere e'lāne <u>sh</u>oru'e sāle jadid az rādyo mi<u>sh</u>and. ba'd do'āye sāle now rā mi<u>kh</u>unand, behamdige tabrik migand o <u>sh</u>irini mi<u>kh</u>orand. dar ayyāme êid mardom be didane hamdige mirand. avval az fāmile nazdik va bozorgāne <u>kh</u>ānevāde <u>sh</u>oru' mikonand o be tadrij be didane hameye dustan o ā<u>sh</u>nāhā mirand. esme in kār did o bāz did-e <u>ch</u>un yeki be didane ādam miād ba'd ādam be bāzdid-e<u>sh</u> mire. marāseme êid betowre kolli sizdah ruz edāme dāre – ruze sizdahome farvardin esme<u>sh</u> sizda-bedar-e. mardom hame az <u>kh</u>unehā<u>sh</u>un birun mirand o dar sahrā vo biābun piknik mikonand. bā in kār nahsiye ruze sizdahom barāye tamāme sāl dar mi<u>sh</u>e.

Vocabulary:

ādam	one; a person	**jam mishand**	they gather
āshnā	acquaintance	**haftsin**	(*see below*)
ayyām	time (*Arabic pl. of* **yowm** = day)	**jadid**	new
		khānevāde	family
		marāsem	ceremonies (*pl. of* **rasm** = custom)
be tadrij	gradually		
betowre kolli	in all, all told		
biābun	wilderness; *anywhere not culti-vated or popu-lated*	**mardom**	people
		mipushand	they wear
		montazere	waiting for
		nahsi	ill luck
		now	new
bozorgān	those who are older, the elders	**sahrā**	fields; desert
		sāl	year
		sare	at
dowre	around	**sofre**	cloth (*see notes*)
dowre ham	together	**shirini**	sweetmeats
êid	festival, feast-day	**shoru'**	beginning
		ta'til	holiday
e'lān	announcement	**tahvil**	hand-over, change-over
fāmil	relatives		

Notes:

sare sofre: Though this phrase can be translated as 'at the table', its literal meaning is 'at the table cloth'. This is because the traditional way of sitting down to eat was, and for many people still is, round a cloth spread on the floor. 'at the table' is **sare miz**. An ordinary table cloth, not intended for eating off, would be **ru mizi**.

haftsin: *literally* the seven s's. The **Now Ruz** table, or cloth, as the case may be, is set with seven things beginning with the Persian letter **sin** (s), as well as a number of other things (such as decorated eggs), each representing desirable elements in the year to come.

sizda-bedar: the traditional outing on the 13th day of the first month of each year, intended to do away with the ill-luck of the 13th days of all the other months. Note that **nahsi** is not used in the sense of 'I had bad luck' – that would be **bad shānsi dāshtam** or **bad shānsi āvordam**; it has an element of superstition as in **ingilisā migand az zire nārdebun nabāyad rad shod, nahs-e** – The English say you shouldn't walk under a ladder, it's bad luck.

nabāyad rad shod: *lit.* you shouldn't pass; impersonal use of **bāyad**, see Lesson 10.

New verbs: **pushidan (push)** – to wear

montazer shodan (shav) – to wait (*note the use of this verb:* **montazere e'lāne shoru'e sāle jadid mishand**)

edāme dāshtan (dār) – to continue

tabrik goftan (gu) – to congratulate

THE CALENDAR

The Iranian calendar is based on the Moslem era. It starts with the flight (or **hejrat**) of the Prophet Mohammed from Mecca to Medina in AD 622. It differs from the Islamic lunar calendar used by the Arab world, however, as it is calculated by the sun and usually has 365 days. It is known as **sāle hejrie shamsi** ('the solar hejira year') and is used for all civil purposes. Religious holidays are observed according to the Islamic calendar (known as **hejrie ghamari**, 'lunar hegira') (see Appendix), so most calendars and diaries will show both sets of dates, together with the corresponding gregorian date. The names of the gregorian calendar months are pronounced as in French, and the Arabic names, with slight variations in one or two cases, are used for the Islamic months.

■ There are twelve months in the Persian calendar year (**sāle iruni davāzdah māh dāre**):

**Farvardin, Ordibehesht, Khordād,
Tir, Mordād, Shahrivar,
Mehr, Ābān, Āzar,
Dey, Bahman, Esfand.**

The first six months have thirty-one days in each, the second five thirty and **Esfand** has twenty nine days and 30 in a leap year. The year begins on the first of **Farvardin** which usually corresponds to

21 March and is the first day of spring. The seasons are reckoned to correspond to three months each, i.e. summer begins with the month of **Tir**, autumn in **Mehr** and winter in **Dey**.

Dates are expressed thus: **avvale farvardine hezāro sisado shasto shish** – the first of Farvardin 1366. When no specific year is mentioned, 'the first of Farvardin' is just **avvale farvardin**.

The corresponding European date would be:

> **bist o yekome mārse hezār o nohsad o**   – 21st March 1987
> **hashtād o haft**

■ THE SEASONS

The seasons are called (**be faslā migand**):

bāhār/bahār	–	spring
tābestun/tābestān	–	summer
pāiz	–	autumn
zemestun/zemestān	–	winter

■ THE DAYS OF THE WEEK
The days are (**be ruzhāye hafte migand**):

shambe	–	Saturday
yekshambe	–	Sunday
doshambe	–	Monday
seshambe	–	Tuesday
chārshambe (chahārshambe)	–	Wednesday
panshambe (panjshambe)	–	Thursday
jom'e	–	Friday

dar Irān ruze jom'e hame jā ta'til-e

■ THE POINTS OF THE COMPASS

The points of the compass are (**be jahāte asliye ghotb-namā migand**):

shomāl, jonub, mashregh, maghreb

and south-east etc. are expressed as follows: **jonube sharghi** (south-east), **shomāle gharbi** (north-west) etc.

TELLING THE TIME

The time is expressed by the use of the word **sā'at** (hour), plus the *ezāfe* plus the cardinal numbers:

sā'ate se	–	three o'clock
sā'ate dah	–	ten o'clock

The word for 'minute' is **daighe/daghighe**; **va/o** is used for 'past', **be** is used for 'to':

sā'ate haft o bist daighe	–	twenty past seven
bist daighe be noh	–	twenty to nine

Half an hour is **nim sā'at** and a quarter of an hour is **ye rob'** or **rob'** or **rob' sā'at**:

sā'ate dah o nim	–	half past ten
sā'ate shish o rob'	–	quarter past six

Note: He came *at* six o'clock = **sā'ate shish āmad**

Examples:

sā'at chand-e?	–	What's the time?
sā'at panje-e	–	It's five o'clock
sā'at panj o panj daighe ast	–	It's five past five
sā'at panj o dah daigh-ast	–	It's ten past five
sā'at panj o rob'-e	–	It's a quarter past five
sā'at panj o bist daigh-ast	–	It's twenty past five
sā'at panj o bist o panj daigh-ast	–	It's twenty-five minutes past five
sā'at panj o nim-e	–	It's half past five
sā'at bist o panj daighe be shish-e	–	It's twenty-five to six
sā'at bist daighe be shish-e	–	It's twenty to six
sā'at ye rob' be shishe-e	–	It's a quarter to six

Note that instead of saying **bist daighe be shish** it is also very common to say **shish o bist daighe kam** i.e. six *less* twenty minutes, **shish o rob' kam** and so on. It is also quite common to leave out the word **sā'at** ('hour') when replying to **sā'at chand-e?**, except for when the time is on the hour:

sā'at panj-e, but **panj o panj daigh-ast, panj o dah daigh-ast, panj o rob'-e, ye rob' be panj-e/panj o rob' kam-e**, *etc.*

The words **zohr** and **nesfe shab** ('midday' and 'midnight') are often used instead of **davāzdah**, though not exclusively. When using **zohr** or **nesfe shab** instead of **sā'ate davāzdah o panj daighe,** or **sā'ate davāzdah o nim**, you would have to say:

panj daighe az zohr/nesfe shab gozashte
nim sā'at az zohr/nesfe shab gozashte
panj daighe be zohr munde, *etc.*

a.m. is usually rendered as **sob**, p.m. as **ba'd az zohr**. If no time is stated, **pish az zohr** refers to the time before noon. Compare the following examples:

sā'ate dahe sob bāyad beram doktor	– I have to go to the doctor at 10 a.m.
sā'ate panje ba'd az zohr biā daftare man	– Come to my office at 5 p.m.
fardā pish az zohr bāyad beram daftare vakilam	– I have to go to my solicitor's office before lunchtime tomorrow

The word **dige/digar** ('other') is used to render the idea of time left, e.g.

ye rob' dige miād	– He'll come in a quarter of an hour
nim sā'at dige kār dāram	– I've got another half an hour's work
shish ruz dige miram mosāferat	– I'll be going away in six days' time
in kār se hafteye dige tamum mishe	– This job will be finished in three weeks' time
otobus dah daigheye dige harekat mikone	– The bus is leaving in ten minutes.

'ago' is rendered by **pish**:

chār sāle pish in sākhtemun injā nabud	– This building wasn't here four years ago

CURRENCY

The basic unit of currency is the **rial** (pronounced *riyal*). Ten rials make one **toman** (toman), and although official monetary figures are always given in rials, and coins and bank notes are both in rials only, native speakers always use the toman for round sums over ten rials, so that whereas, for example, a ministry might declare that they had budgeted one million rials for some purchase or other, a private individual would always refer to the same sum as one hundred thousand tomans (**sad ezār/hezār toman**). Till slips, receipts, etc. are always in rials, but in handing you a bill for 1500 rials, the shop assistant will say **sad o panjā toman** or **sad o panjā toman mishe**.

In speech, the words **gherun** (usually only used for one single rial) and **ezār**, or **zār** after a number ending in a vowel sound, are used to mean rial, although in fact they are survivors of older currency systems. You will therefore hear the following:

> **ye-gherun** – 1 rial
> **do zār** – 2 rials
> **se zār, chārezār, panjezār, shishezār, hafezār, hashezār, nozār, ye toman; yāzdezār, davāzdezār, sizdezār, chārdezār, punzdezār, shunzdezār, hivdezār, hizhdezār, nuzdezār, do toman; bist o ye-gherun, bisto do zar** *etc.* until **se toman**. From this point on it is usual to say **se toman o ye-gherun, se toman o do zār, se toman o se zār**, etc.

Change is called **pule khurd** and notes are **eskenās**.

A list of coins and notes currently in circulation is given in the Appendix.

▌EXPRESSIONS OF TIME:

che sā'ati miād?	–	At what time is he coming?
sā'ate doye ba'd az zohr	–	2 p.m.
sā'ate seye ba'd az nesfe shab	–	3 a.m. (*You can also say* **seye sob**, *but the hours nearer midnight tend to be referred to rather than to the morning*)

mähe gozashté	–	Last month
säle gozashté/parsal	–	Last year
shambeye pish	–	Last Saturday
shambeye gozashté	–	Last Saturday
doshambeye äyande	–	Next Monday
doshambeye dige	–	Next Monday
sare zohr	–	At noon, on the dot of noon
sare shab	–	Early evening (*different use of the word* sare)
cherä dir kardi?	–	Why are you late?
ma'zerat mikhäm ke dir kardam	–	I'm sorry I'm late
bebakhshid ke dir kardam	–	I'm sorry I'm late
mesle inke zud ämadam	–	It looks as though I'm early
dir nayä	–	Don't be late
sä'atam khäbidé	–	My watch has stopped
sä'ate män aghab-e/jelo-e	–	My watch is slow/fast

EXERCISES

A. Read aloud and translate into English:

Maryam ye ketäb däre. emruz Hasan behesh dotä daftar däd. shambe Maryam be madrese mire. madreseye Maryam bozorg-e. taghriban haftsadtä shägerd däre. dar har keläs hodude chehceltä shägerd hast. dar Irän bachchehä faghat jom'e ta'til-and. az shambe tä chärshambe bishtare madresehä sä'ate käreshun az hashte sob tä yek o nime ba'd az zohr-e. panjshambehä faghat tä daväzda hastand. säle tahsili az avvale mehr shoru' mishe va ma'mulan tä aväkhere khordäd yeksare edäme dare. faghat dar avvale bahär ham baräye eîde now ruz sizda ruz ta'tili därand.

New words:	shägerd	pupil
	säle tahsili	the academic year
	ma'mulan	usually
	aväkher	around the end (of); *pl. of* äkhar, the end
	yeksare	straight through
	edäme däre	it continues

B. Put into Persian:

1. He's coming on Saturday
2. It's twenty past seven
3. I have a meeting at eight o'clock
4. My exams are in six months' time (use *emtahān dāshtan*)
5. I'm going to England on business next month
6. I have to be at the airport by seven a.m.
7. They left for London at eight p.m. yesterday
8. What time does the train leave?
9. Please don't be late because I have a lot to do
10. I worked every day last week
11. Don't you have any change?
12. The seventh of Ordibehesht 1366.

Lesson Nine
(darse nohom)

Read aloud:

■ salām, Maryam, hālet chetowr-e?

to-i, Susan, salām, khêili vaght-e nadidamet – kojā-i?

haminjāhā. faghat diruz o pariruz dāneshgāh nayumadam chun mādaram mariz bud.

chetowr, mage kese digei nabud pishesh bemune?

na, nabud. khob, che khabar, diruz chikar kardin?

mā kāre ziādi nakardim. ostāde jadid umadé bud bā hame āshnā beshe. modatti ham tuye kelāse mā bud.

adabiyyāt dars mide?

na, tārikh

emtahān chi shod?

māle mā bad nabud vali shenidam māle goruhe to khêili sakht bud.

pas che behtar ke man nabudam. rāsti khabar nadāri rājebe ketābkhune chikar kardand?

hanuz ke hichchi. migand khode ra'ise dāneshgā ham nemidune

<u>ch</u>ikār kone. albatte benazare man bāyad tuye ta'tilāt-am vāz bā<u>sh</u>e
vali <u>kh</u>ob, lābod sarparasti<u>sh</u> mo<u>sh</u>kel mi<u>sh</u>e
āre, in ke hast. rāsti, tā yādam narafté, in pu<u>sh</u>e māle to-e?
e – āre, <u>ch</u>e <u>kh</u>ub, fekr mikardam <u>sh</u>āyad injāhā oftādé bā<u>sh</u>e,
<u>kh</u>êɪli mamnun
ey vāy – sā'at o negā kon! bāyad beram – <u>kh</u>êɪli dir <u>sh</u>od, <u>gh</u>orbāne
to
<u>kh</u>odāfez

Vocabulary:

adabiyyāt	literature	**<u>kh</u>ode ra'is**	the head himself
ā<u>sh</u>nā <u>sh</u>odan	to get acquainted	**ra'is**	director, boss
<u>ch</u>e behtar	so much the better	**modatti**	a while
		nadidamet	= *to ro nadidé-am*
<u>ch</u>ikār (*che kar*)	what	**ostād**	professor (*also* s.o. good at sth.)
<u>ch</u>ikār kardin (*coll.* for **kardid**)	what did you do	**pu<u>sh</u>e**	folder
emtahān	exam	**rājebe** (*raje'be*)	about
goruh	group	**sarparasti**	supervision
<u>gh</u>orbāne to	goodbye (see Lesson 12)	**Susan**	girl's name
kāre ziādi nakardim	we didn't do much	**tārikh**	history
ketāb<u>kh</u>une	library, bookshelf	**tā'tilāt-am**	*short form of* **tā'tilāt ham**

PRONOUNS

Personal pronouns, subject pronouns and the pronominal suffixes
have already been mentioned in Lesson Two.

Other pronouns are as follows:

1. Possessive Pronouns (mine, yours, etc)

The possessive pronouns are rendered in Persian by the use of the word **māle**, 'belonging to', and the personal pronoun:

un ketāb māle man-e	–	That book is mine
in kife pul māle to-st?	–	Is this purse yours?
pedaram ke<u>sh</u>āvarz-e,	–	My father's a farmer, the
trāktor māle un-e		tractor is his
mā<u>sh</u>ine kerem māle mā-st	–	The cream-coloured car is ours
in ru sari māle <u>sh</u>omā-st?	–	Is this headscarf yours?
otā<u>gh</u> ku<u>ch</u>ikè* māle unā-st	–	The little room is theirs

***otā<u>gh</u> ku<u>ch</u>ikè:** see Colloquial Use of the *ezāfe*, below.

2. Interrogative Pronouns

The word **ki?** renders 'who?', 'whom', in colloquial Persian. It is considered to be definite and therefore takes **rā** when it is the direct object of the verb:

ki umad?	–	Who came?
ki bud?	–	Who was it?
kiy-e	–	Who is it?
kiyo did?	–	Whom did he see?
kiyo zad?	–	Whom did he hit?

3. Indefinite Pronouns

(a) **hame** – all, everyone
hame umadand – They all came, everyone came

hame is often used with the *ezāfe*, to indicate possession:
hameye dāne<u>sh</u>juyān dars   All (of) the students study,
mi<u>kh</u>unand   *or* all students study

hame also takes the pronominal suffix **-a<u>sh</u>** in the third person, to give **hamea<u>sh</u>/hama<u>sh</u>** – all of it:
āsemun hama<u>sh</u> ābi bud	– The sky was all blue
<u>gh</u>azā <u>kh</u>ub bud? bale, hama<u>sh</u>	– Was the food good? Yes,
o <u>kh</u>ordam	I ate it all (all of it)

hama**sh** is also used to mean 'all the time':

Engelestān havā**sh** hi**ch khub** nist, hama**sh** bārun miād (hava**sh** = havāya**sh**) – English weather isn't at all good, it rains all the time

(b) kesi – someone; no-one (*with a negative verb*)
hi**ch**kas – no one

kesi unjāst?	–	Is anyone there?
kesi hast?	–	Is anyone there?
kesi nist	–	There's no one (there)
hi**ch**kas nist	–	There's no one (there)
hi**ch**ki nabud	–	There was no one (there)

hi**ch** kudum – none

hi**ch** kudum az in **ch**izā ro nemikhām	I don't want any of these things
hi**ch** kudum az in na**ghsh**ehā bedard nemi**kh**orand	None of these maps is any good

Note that Persian uses the double negative in such cases.

(c) tamāme – the whole of, all

tamāme **sh**ab kār kard	–	He worked all night
tamāme ruz jalese dā**sh**tim	–	We had meetings all day

(d) dige/digar – another

hamdige	–	one another
yekdige	–	one another
be hamdige salām kardand	–	They greeted one another

(e) folān, folāni – so-and-so

folān kas	–	So-and-so
folāni umad	–	So-and-so came
folāni ostāde in kār-e	–	So-and-so is very good at this

(f) **ba'zi** – some
This precedes the noun it qualifies, which is put in the plural
and does not take the *ezāfe*:

ba'zi ketābā khub nistand –	Some books are not good
dar ba'zi jāhā havā khêili	The weather has got very cold
sard shode	in some places

Note the difference in the use of **ba'zi** and **chandtā**. **chandtā**
carries the sense that a few individual items or people are
referred to:

I bought some books – **chandtā ketāb kharidam**

ba'zi is also used as a noun, in which case it takes **az**:

ba'zi az unhā	–	Some of them
ba'zi az kārkhunehā emruz	–	Some of the factories are
ta'til-and		closed today
ba'zihā neshastand, ba'zihā	–	Some people sat down,
pā shodand		others got up
ba'zihā az kār kardan	–	Some people don't like
khosheshun nemiād		working

khosh āmadan (ā), 'to like', takes the pronominal suffixes:
az Irān khosham miād – I like Iran

bad āmadan, 'to dislike', behaves in the same way:
az ādame durughgu badam miād – I don't like people who
tell lies

(g) **kam**: few, little
kami: a few, a little
yek kami: a little

ghazā kam bud – The food was not enough
kami āb mikhām – I want a little water (some water)
ye kami āb mikhām – I want a little water (some water)

4. Khod

In colloquial Persian the word **khod** which basically means 'self' is mainly used in the following ways:

(a) with the pronominal suffixes (**-am, -at, -ash; -emān, -etān, -eshan**) and **rā** to form a kind of reflexive:

khodet o khaste nakon (khodat rā khaste nakon)	– Don't tire yourself
khodet o nārāhat nakon	– Don't upset yourself/ Don't get upset

(b) when the possessive adjective or personal pronoun refers to the subject of the sentence, the word **khod** is used, and in colloquial usage, it is again used with the pronominal suffixes:

ghalame khodesh o beman dād – He gave me his own pen

(c) **khod** is also used as an emphatic particle, with the *ezāfe*:

khode u bud – It was he himself

which colloquially will be: **khodesh bud**

dar khode Landan zendegi mikone – He lives in London itself

Here are some more examples:

khodesh dar o bāz kard	– She opened the door herself
khodam miram	– I'll go myself
khodet bokon	– Do it yourself!
cherā khodet nemiri?	– Why don't you go yourself?
khodesh khāst	– He himself/she herself wanted (it)

5. Colloquial Use of Pronominal Suffixes

In Lesson Two we saw the use of the pronominal suffixes: **-am, -esh, -et, -emun, -etun, -eshun**, to convey the possessive: **ketābam, ketābesh,** *etc*. This use is extended to a variety of other expressions which, in English, would not qualify as possessives:

dishab ye restorāne tāze raftim, ghazāsh khêıli khub bud	– We went to a new restaurant last night, the food was very good

hendunash khêili khub-e, mikhāi – ye kami behet bedam?	This water melon's very good, do you want some?
in ghazā namakesh khêili ziād-e –	There's too much salt in this food
in naghghāsh kāresh khêili khub-e –	This painter's work is very good

(See also the example about the weather under 3(a): havāsh)

Yet another use of these suffixes is instead of the personal pronouns plus rā:

uno shenākhtam (u rā shenākhtam) – I recognised him/her
so that we have shenākhtamesh

khêili vaght-e nadidamet – I haven't seen you for a long time/for ages

In compound verbs, the suffixes are usually added to the noun/adjective element of the verb, though compounds with prepositions tend to vary:

māshinet chi shod?	– What happened about your car?
dorostesh kardam (un o dorost kardam)	– I fixed it
barāt nāme umade bud, didish?	– There was a letter for you, did you see it?
āre, bar dāshtamesh	– Yes, I picked it up
āre, baresh dāshtam	– Yes, I picked it up

COLLOQUIAL USE OF THE EZĀFE

One of the examples given in (1) above was:
otāgh kuchikè māle unā-st – The little room is theirs

You would expect this to have been otāghe kuchik māle unā-st, but in ordinary conversation, when a definite noun is qualified by an adjective, it is very common for the *ezāfe* to move onto the adjective *and* to take the stress:

āchār bozorgè kojā-st? – Where's the big spanner

nemidunam, tāzegi nadidame<u>sh</u>	– I don't know, I haven't
vali ku<u>ch</u>ikè ruye miz-e	seen it lately but the little
	one's on the table.

If the noun in such a phrase is the direct object, taking **rā**, there is a further change:

ā<u>ch</u>ār bozorgàro kojā	– Where did you put the big
gozā<u>sh</u>ti? (è becomes à)	spanner?
kif siāhàmo nadidi?	– Have you seen my black bag?

Notice that in Persian we say **nadidi** where in English a straight-forward 'have you seen' is more natural. 'haven't you seen' (indicating that you might well have been expected to have done) is also **nadidi**, but with a different intonation.

CONJUNCTIONS

The most common conjunctions are:

va/o: and
ham: also, and
ham . . . va ham: both . . . and
yā: or
yā . . . yā: either . . . or
na . . . va na: neither . . . nor
vali, ammā: but
mage/magar: but; with a negative verb, **mage** has the meaning 'didn't . . .?'

Most of the above have already been encountered in the reading passages and examples, but here are some further examples:

kāretun o tamum kardid? bale, ham nāmehāye emruz o mā<u>sh</u>in kardam o ham māle diruz o –
Have you finished your work? Yes, I typed both yesterday's letters and today's

yeki az inā ro bāyad entekhāb konid, yā in yā un –
You must choose one of these, either this one or that one

na az in <u>kh</u>o<u>sh</u>am miād na az un, or na az in <u>kh</u>o<u>sh</u>am miād na az un yeki –
I like neither this one nor that one

in restorän ghazāsh khub-e, vali māle un yeki behtar-e –
The food in this restaurant is good, but the food in that one is
better
mikhāstam barāt gol biāram ammā golforushi baste bud –
I wanted to bring you some flowers, but the florist's was shut
mage nadidi māshin az kudum taraf miāmad? –
Didn't you see which way the car was coming?

■ PHRASES AND EXPRESSIONS

bedard khordan	To be useful
bedardam nemikhore	It's no use to me
bedardet mikhore?	Is it any use to you?
bedard nemikhore	It's no good; it's no use (of things)
fāyede nadāre	It's no use (figurative)
velesh kon	Leave it alone (un o vel kon)
velam kon	Leave me alone
shomāhā	You people, you lot
khod be khod	Of its own accord

Proverbs

ham khodā ro mikhād ham khormā ro	He wants to have his cake and eat it (lit. he wants both God and the date)
bā do tir ye neshun (zadan)	To kill two birds with one stone (lit. with two shots, one target)
siliye naghd beh az halvāye nesy-ast (nesye ast)	A bird in the hand is worth two in the bush (lit. a slap in cash is better than halva on account)
ham fāl o ham tamāsha	Business and pleasure

EXERCISES

A. *Read aloud and translate:*
1. un khodnevis o bar nadār, māle man-e
2. bishtare in zaminhā māle dowlat-e
3. age gofti diruz kiyo didam
4. harche dar zadam hichki javāb nadād
5. diruz tamāme vaght dars khundam

6. khodnevis siāhèye man o nadidi?
   khodnevise siāham o nadidi?
7. emsāl barāye êid mikhām beram kenāre daryā – shenidam un
   vaghte sāl havāsh khêili khub-e
8. in kār khêili āsun-e, chetowr khodet nemikonish
9. mage nemidunesti emruz hame jā tā'til-e?
10. hichvaght in kār o nakon, khêili badam miād

B. Put into Persian
1. There was no one there
2. Why didn't you go yourself? (*give polite and familiar forms*)
3. Have you seen my white bag?
4. That restaurant's food is very bad
5. What did you do about your car? I fixed it
6. Don't take that folder, it's mine
7. I don't like any of these shoes
8. I was on the plane all night
9. Some shops are closed tomorrow
10. She came in her own car

Lesson Ten
(darse dahom)

Read aloud:
■ (bā sedāye boland bekhunid)
                    shahrhāye Irān

mohemtarin shahre Irān Tehrān-e, ke pāyetakhte keshvar o
markaze hokumate. khêili az kārkhunehāye bozorg o kuchik ham
dar atrāfe Tehrān ghharār gereftand. shahrhāye mohemme digeye
Irān Mashhad, Tabriz, Esfahān o Shirāz-and. Mashhad, ke dar
shomāle sharghiye Irān ast, shahre ziārati-st chun ghabre Emām
Rezā, emāme hashtome shi'ayān dar unjā-st. havāye Mashhad
khonaktar az havāye Tehrān-e va mardom aghlab dar tābestun
barāye ziārat o gardesh be unjā miran. nazdike Mashhad, dar Tus,

ghabre Ferdowsi, shā'ere bozorge irāni gharār gerefté ke shāyad tarjomeye ash'āre u rā khundé bāshid. agar javāher dust dāshté bāshid, firuzeye Mashhad niz ma'ruf ast.

Tabriz bozorgtarin shahre shomāle gharbiye Irān-e va mardome unjā dar asl tork zabān hastand. albatte hame fārsi ham harf mizanand chun dar madāres fārsi tadris mishe. agar ādam bekhād az rāhe zamini be Orupā bere, ma'mulan az Tabriz rad mishe va bishtare tejārate zaminiye bêine Irān o Orupā niz az rāhe Tabriz anjām mishe chun alāve bar jādde, khatte asliye rāhāhan niz az unjā rad mishe. Tabriz dāneshgāhe bozorgi dāre. ghāli va noghre-kāriye in shahr ham ma'ruf ast.

Vocabulary:

aghlab	generally	**mohem**	important
alāve bar	in addition to	**shā'er**	poet
ash'ār	poems (*pl. of* she'r)	**shi'ayān**	*pl. of* shi'e, Shiites, the sect of Islam which is the official religion of Iran
dust dāshtan	to like		
emām	religious leader		
firuze	turquoise		
ghabr	grave	**tadris**	teaching
ghāli	carpet	**tarjome**	translation
gharār gerefté	is situated	**tejārat**	trade
hokumat	government	**tork**	Turkish, Turk
javāher	jewel	**tork-zabān**	Turkish-speaking
ke	that		
madāres	*pl. of* madrese	**zabān**	tongue
markaz	centre	**zamini**	overland
ma'ruf	famous	**ziārat**	pilgrimage

SUBORDINATE CLAUSES

1. Relative Clauses

Relative clauses are generally introduced by the relative pronoun

ke which in this context will mean 'that', 'which', 'who', 'whom' *etc*. The unaccented suffix **i** is then usually added to the noun beginning the relative expression (the antecedent).

In this context, this **i** which we have already encountered as an indefinite suffix (**ketābi** – a book) has the effect of singling out the noun and making it definite:

ketābi ke kharidam khub nabud	– The book that I bought wasn't any good
khānumi ke poshte miz bud ingilisi balad nabud	– The lady behind the desk didn't know any English
yād dāshti ro ke be u dādam gom kard	– He lost the note I gave him

Nouns already ending in **i** do not take another one:

sandali ke āvord shekaste bud – The chair he brought was broken

Note, however, that proper nouns and nouns with personal endings indicating the possessive do not take the suffix **i**:

Hasan ke ketābesho beman gharz dād dāneshju bud – Hassan, who lent me his book, was a student

Mashhad, ke dar shomāle sharghiye Irān-e, shahre bozorgiy-e – Mashad, which is in the north east of Iran, is a big city

un barādaram ke tuye sherkate naft kār mikone rafté Ahvāz – My brother who works in the oil company has gone to Ahwaz

2. Indirect Statements

Indirect statements, questions and reported speech will also be introduced by **ke**:

sābkhune goft ke shām hāzer-e	– The hostess said that supper was ready
porsid ke istgāhe otobus kojā-st	– He asked where the bus stop was
gārāzh behem goft ke māshinam hanuz hāzer nist	– The garage told me that my car wasn't ready yet

Notice the difference in the use of tenses in Persian and English, as reported speech in Persian is in the same tense as would have been used in the original statement. If in doubt about which tense to use, think what the original statement would be and use the same tense in the subordinate clause.

3. Wishes and Commands

(a)   The subordinate clause in wishes and commands is introduced by **ke** followed by the verb in the subjunctive:

>**behesh goft ke bere** (*beravad*) **nun bekhare** – He told him to go and buy some bread
>**azesh khāst ke biād o bā khodesh motarjem biāre** – He asked him to come and bring an interpreter with him
>**beman goft ke zud biām kārhā ro shoru' konam** – She told me to come early and start the work

(b)   'I wish . . .' referring to the future can be said in two ways, either:

(i)   with **kāshki/kāsh ke** and the verb in the subjunctive:
>**kāshki biād** – I wish he would come/I do hope he'll come

or:

(ii)   with **khodā kone ke/khodā konad ke** plus the subjunctive:
>**khodā kone ke biād** – I do hope he'll come (*lit.* may God make him to come)

>**khodā nakone** – God forbid – is used as an interjection and also with the subjunctive like **khodā kone**

For the past, **kāshki** is used with the imperfect or pluperfect:

kāshki umadé bud	–	I wish he had come
kāshki in kār-o nakardé budam	–	I wish I hadn't done that

4. Result Clauses

These are introduced:

(a)   by **unghadr** ('so much') and **untowr** ('like that') in the main clause, plus **ke** to introduce the next clause with the verb in the present or past tense for definite consequences, and in the subjunctive for indefinite consequences:

unghadr khub sheno kard ke mosābegharo bord – He swam so well that he won the race

shāgerd darsesh o unghadr khub balad nabud ke ghabul beshe – The pupil didn't know his subject well enough to pass

man u rā unghadr khub nemishnāsam ke in o behesh begam – I don't know him well enough to tell him this

havā untowr ham nist ke beshe bedune pālto birun raft – The weather isn't really such that you can go out without a coat

Note that where **unghadr** is used in a time context, for example to mean 'so often', 'so long' etc., then it is used with **tā** and does not take the subjunctive:

unghadr telefon kardam tā belakhare giresh āvordam – I kept on telephoning until I got hold of him

(b) by **tā** ('so that', 'in order to') which usually takes the subjunctive:

man kār mikonam tā zendegiye behtari dāshte bāsham – I work so that I can have a better life

ajalle kard tā be teran berese (*beresad*) – She hurried in order to get the train.

(c) colloquially, by **ke**:

panjere ro baz kard ke havā biād – He opened the window to let in some air

zud āmadam ke to rā ghabl az raftan bebinam – I came early so that I could see you before leaving

(d) by **barāye inke**. In addition to 'because', **barāye inke** can also mean 'in order that' in which case it takes the subjunctive and usually comes at the beginning of the sentence:

barāye inke betunam khune bekharam, meghdāre bishtari pul lāzem dāram – I need more money in order to be able to buy a house.

You could also say:

meghdāre bishtari pul lāzem dāram tā betunam khune bekharam

5. Conditional Sentences

Conditional sentences are generally introduced by **agar** ('if') and can be divided into those referring to possible conditions and those referring to impossible conditions.

(a) Impossible conditions

Sentences referring to impossible conditions generally take the imperfect tense in both parts:

agar midunestam ke hāzer nisti nemiumadam – I wouldn't have come if I'd known you weren't ready
agar fārsi balad budam in ketāb-o nemikharidam – If I knew Persian, I wouldn't have bought this book
agar zud miāmad bā ham miraftim kharid – If he had come early, we'd have gone shopping together

(b) Possible conditions

(i) Sentences expressing a straightforward possibility, with little element of doubt, take the present tense in the 'if' clause and the present or future tense in the other clause:

agar khāb-e, bidaresh nakon	– If he's asleep, don't wake him
agar motma'en nisti, nakon	– Don't do it if you're not sure
agar kār dāri, nayā	– Don't come if you're busy
agar kharāb-e behesh dast nazan	– Don't touch it if it's not working

(ii) Possible conditions referring to the future (where there is, therefore, much more of an element of doubt) take the present subjunctive in the 'if' clause:

agar biād bā ham mirim bāzār – If he comes, we'll go to the bazaar together
agar in kāro barāye man bekoni, khêili mamnunet misham – If you do this for me I'll be very grateful to you

agar havā <u>kh</u>ub bā<u>sh</u>e mirim birun – We'll go out if the weather's good

agar rāh o gom nakonam, zud miresam – I'll get there quickly if I don't lose the way

agar beman begi <u>ch</u>i lāzem dari, barāt mi<u>kh</u>aram – If you tell me what you need, I'll buy it for you

When, however, the action in the 'if' clause is a single action which precedes the action in the main clause, the simple past is used:

agar telefon kard, begu ke man manzel nistam – If he telephones, tell him that I'm not at home

agar dustam umad in nāme ro behe<u>sh</u> bede – If my friend comes, give her this letter

agar rafti mosāferat hatman barām nāme benevis – Do write to me if you go away

(iii) When the 'if' clause refers to the past, the past subjunctive is used:

agar otobus rafté bā<u>sh</u>e dirtar miresam – If the bus has left I'll arrive later

(iv) When **magar** or **magar inke** is used conditionally (to mean 'unless'), it takes the verb in the subjunctive:

man unjā nemiram magar inke to ham bāhem biāi – I won't go there unless you come with me

6. Possibility

In addition to the use of **<u>sh</u>āyad** (Lesson Four), possibility is also expressed by the use of **momken ast ke** followed by the verb in the subjunctive.

Colloquially this becomes **momken-e** and **ke** is often omitted:

momken-e biād	–	He may come
momken-e tasādof kardé bā<u>sh</u>e	–	He may have had an accident
momken-e fardā havā <u>kh</u>ub bā<u>sh</u>e	–	It may be fine tomorrow

The same construction can also be used for polite requests:

momken-e in kār o barāye man bekoni? – Can you possibly do this for me

momken-e beporsam <u>chi</u> sho<u>dé</u> – May I ask what's happened?

momken-e beman begid nazdiktarin istgāhe otobus kojā-st – Could you tell me where the nearest bus stop is?

IMPERSONAL CONSTRUCTIONS

Look again at the fourth sentence in 4(a) above:

havā untowr ham nist ke *be<u>sh</u>e* bedune pālto *birun raft*

bāyad and the appropriate tenses of **<u>sh</u>odan** can be used with the past stem to give an impersonal construction:

bāyad raft	–	One/you must go, it is necessary to go
mi<u>sh</u>e raft	–	It is possible to go, you/one can go
mi<u>sh</u>e goft (ke)	–	It can be said (that) . . .

tavānestan can also be used in this way, but not colloquially.

■ PHRASES AND EXPRESSIONS

na bābā	You don't say
age gofti/agar gofti	(*lit.* if you said) do you know what, guess what
bāyad sā<u>kh</u>t	(*lit.* one has to build) one must make do, one must adapt. **sā<u>kh</u>tan** *also has the meaning of* to make do with, to get along with
misāzim, dige	Well, we manage
age beduni/agar beduni	You've no idea . . .; *e.g.* **age beduni <u>ch</u>e<u>gh</u>adr in kār sa<u>kh</u>t bud** you've no idea how difficult this was

fekr nakonam + *subjunctive*, **gamān nakonam** (+ *subjunctive*)	I don't think . . . *Very often used instead of* **fekr nemikonam ke** . . . *which also takes the subjunctive.*
fekr nakonam biād **khosh gozasht**	I don't think he'll come (*lit.* it passed well) I/we had a good time *e.g.* **dishab raftim mehmuni, khêli khosh gozasht** we went to a party last night, we enjoyed ourselves very much. **khosh gozashtan** *is conjugated in the third person only and is used impersonally*: **khosh migzare/migozarad?** are you having a good time?

EXERCISES

A. Read aloud and translate:

1. azam khāst ke biām
2. mosāfer porsid ke havāpêima che sā'ati parvāz mikone
3. bachche unghadre gerye kard ta khābesh bord
4. agar bekhāy (bekhāhi) mitunam biām aghabet bebaramet kharid
5. agar beman gofté budi ke māshin nadāri zudtar miāmadam
6. jā dārid agar bekhām yek shab ezāfe bemunam?
7. momkene fardā nakhām beram birun
8. panjeraro unghadr mohkam bast ke shishash shikast
9. agar khub kār koni zud pishraft mikoni (pishraft = *progress*)
10. agar diruz bā mā miāmadi behet khosh migozasht

B. Put into Persian

1. He told me he was going to stay at home all day
2. She said that she would try and find my purse
3. He asked me what I was going to do
4. I thought you were coming yesterday
5. If I'd known you had this book, I wouldn't have bought it
6. If he comes, tell him I've gone

7. Can you tell me where I can find a chemist?
8. Will it be ready if I come tomorrow?
9. I don't think that's right
10. Will I be able to see the doctor if I wait?

Lesson Eleven
(darse yāzdahom)

Read aloud:
(bā sedāye boland bekhunid)
shahrhāye Irān

barāye khārejihā ruzi Esfahān ma'ruftarin shahre keshvar bud chun dar zamāne pādeshāhāne safaviyye ke taghriban hamdowreye Elizābete avval budand, pāyetakhte mamlekat bud. Esfahān ke dar kenāre Zāyande rud ghārār gerefté chand masjede ma'rufe besyār didani dāre va mêidāne shahr hanuz az mêidānhāye mashhure donyāst. ghāli, dastduzi, noghre-kāri, khātam-kāri va shiriniye makhsusi benāme gaz hame az towlidāte mohemme in shahr-and. agar az bāzār didan konid mitunid bishtare inhā rā dar hāle dorost shodan bebinid.

shahre Shirāz hodude chārsad kilometriye jonube Esfahān ghārār gerefté. maghbarehāye Hāfez o Sa'di, do shā'ere bozorge digeye irāni, dar Shirāz ast va khode shahr ham zibā o didani-st. bāghhāye besyār ghashang va bāzāre jālebi ham dāre. albatte barāye mosāfer shāyad az hame chiz jālebtar didane āsāre bāstāniye takhte jamshid va naghshe rostam bāshe ke dar nazdikiye Shirāz ghārār gerefté.

bishtare manāteghe naftkhize Irān dar jonub-and va sahme omdeye darāmade keshvar az san'ate naft bedast miād. sābeghan pālāyesh-gāhe Ābādān az bozorgtarin pālāyeshgāhāye donyā bud. sāderāte naft az tarighe Khalije Fārs surat migire va zendegiye mardome in ghesmat az keshvar aksaran be san'ate naft vābastegi dāre. shahre Bandar Abbās albatte betowre kolli bandare tejāriye bozorgiye va e kheili az kālāhāike az rāhe daryā be Irān miānd be unjā vāred mishan.

Vocabulary:

āsār	remains (*pl. of* asar)	ma'ruf	famous
bandar	port	mashhur	famous
bāstāni	ancient	naftkhiz	oil producing
darāmad	income	omde	main, major
didani	worth seeing	pādeshāh	king
hamdowre	contemporary	rud	river
jāleb	interesting	Takhte Jamshid	Persepolis
kālā	goods	towlidāt	products
khārej	abroad	sāderāt	exports
khātam-kāri	inlaid work	sahm	share
maghbare	tomb	san'at	industry
manātegh	regions (*pl. of* mantaghe)	vābastegi dāre	depends on
		zamān	age, time

WORD FORMATION

Comprehensive explanations of all the various word formations are beyond the scope of this book. A few of the more common variations are mentioned here as they should help you to understand what you might hear.

1. Abstract Nouns
Abstract nouns are formed by the addition of an accented i to the adjective:

khub	–	khubi (goodness)
bad	–	badi (evil)
tambal	–	tambali (laziness)
zerang	–	zerangi (cleverness)
bad bakht	–	bad bakhti (misfortune)

Where the adjective ends in the sound **e**, a **g** is added for euphony between the **e** and the **i** ending:

khaste	–	**khastegi** (weariness)
gorosne	–	**gorosnegi** (hunger)
teshne	–	**teshnegi** (thirst)

The stress on the **i** ending of abstract nouns is what distinguishes it from the indefinite **i** ending.

Read the following aloud and notice the difference:

marde khubi	–	a good man
khubiye mard	–	the man's goodness

2. Verbal Nouns

Verbal nouns are formed by the addition of various suffixes to the present stem. The most easily distinguishable of these is the suffix **-esh**:

kushidan (kush)	–	**kushesh** (effort)
sukhtan (suz)	–	**suzesh** (a burning sensation)
khāridan (khār)	–	**khāresh** (itching)
bakhshidan (bakhsh)	–	**bakhshesh** (forgiveness)
pushidan (push)	–	**pushesh** (covering – *a word now often heard in the context of* **pusheshe eslāmi** *which refers to suitable Islamic dress*)

3. The Causative

In colloquial Persian the addition of the suffix **-āndan** to the present stem of the verb gives what is known as the causative verb (because it has the meaning of making something happen). This new verb takes the usual personal endings:

residan (res) – **resāndan** (to cause to arrive)

dustam man-o bā māshinesh resund khune – My friend took me home in his car

4. *The Gerundive*

shahre Shirāz zibā va didani-st – Shiraz is beautiful and worth seeing

The addition of an unaccented **i** suffix to the infinitive of some verbs gives what is known as the gerundive which has the meaning of 'to be done', 'worth doing':

didani	–	worth seeing
raftani	–	due to go, being about to go, having to go
shodani	–	do-able
shenidani	–	worth hearing
sedāye bolbol shenidani-st	–	The song of the nightingale is worth hearing
in kār shodani nist	–	This cannot be done

The gerundive of **mordan**, to die, is often heard in the context of **lāghar o mordani** for people or animals that are thin and sickly-looking, or just very thin and therefore look as if they are about to die. You would not say **mordani** of a person who really was about to die.

5. *Diminutives* are formed by the addition of the following suffixes to the noun:

-ak	–	**pesarak, dokhtarak, mardak, zanak, teflak** (**tefl** = infant)
-e	–	**pesare, dokhtare, marde, zane**
-eke	–	**mardeke** (*coll.* **martike**), **zaneke** (*coll.* **zanike**)
-che	–	**baghche**
-iche	–	**dariche**

When these suffixes are added to nouns denoting people they can also denote either affection or contempt. When used for adults they are quite often somewhat rude or contemptuous, but it should also be noted that different suffixes will give a different shade of meaning to the same word, for example:

dokhtarak and **pesarak** usually convey the straightforward diminutive meaning and can be used affectionately, **teflak** is very common and just means 'poor thing' but:

dokhtare, pesare, are usually slightly pejorative, and

mardak, zanak, are used in a slightly derogatory sense or are at best disrespectful, with **martike** and **zanike** being downright rude, whereas **marde, zane**, while not altogether polite, will often be heard in speech and mean little more than 'the man', 'that man', 'the woman', 'that woman':

raftam nunvāi marde goft ke nun tamum shodé – I went to the bakery and the man said the bread was finished

If one wants to be more polite, one refers to **āghāhe, khānume**.

Otherwise one should say **un āghā, un khānum**, for 'that man', 'that woman'.

6. *Colloquial use of the suffix -esh*

The suffix **-esh** is also used colloquially as a kind of pronominal suffix where none is actually needed:

harchi aghabe dustam gashtam nabudesh
This is given here so that you will recognize it if you hear it.

7. *Other word formations*

(*a*)   The suffixes **-gar** and **-chi** tend to denote occupations:

kārgar – worker; **zargar** – goldsmith; **āhangar** – blacksmith; **shenogar** – swimmer; **shekārchi** – hunter

(*b*)   nouns can be formed from two nouns put together as in:
ruznāme – newspaper; **mehmānkhāne** – hotel; **davākhāne** – chemist

or from the combination of a noun and a verb:
piāderow – pavement; **sarbāz** – soldier; **kārkonān** – workers

or by the combination of a preposition and a noun:
hamsafar – fellow-traveller; **hambāzi** – playmate; **hamrāh** – companion

(*c*)   prepositions and nouns can also give adjectives:

bikār – unemployed; **biadab** – rude

EXERCISES

A. Read aloud and translate:
1. kāresh-o bā zerangi pish bord
2. az gorosnegi o teshnegi dāsht mimord
3. bedune pusheshe eslāmi tuye kuche nabāyad raft
4. agar teran-o az dast dādi khodam bā māshin miresunamet
5. dar Orupā shahrhāye didani khêili ziād ast
6. sedāye in khānandeye jadid vāghe'an shenidani-st
7. belakhare nafahmidam ke in kār shodani-st yā na
8. diruz raftam aghabe sā'atam, marde goft ke hāzer nist
9. rānandehe cherāgh ghermez-o nadid, zad be ye māshine dige
10. dokhtare khêili por ru bud

B. Put into Persian
1. I am extremely tired (*say*: I am dying of tiredness)
2. You won't get the job done by being lazy
3. Shiraz is beautiful and worth seeing
4. I wanted to change the door of my house but the man said it couldn't be done
5. My friend said she would take me home
6. The little boy was very tired
7. That [awful] boy stuck his tongue out at me (*use* zabun derazi kardan)
8. The poor little thing is very tired

C. Give the opposites of: khubi; zerangi; khosh-bakhti

Lesson Twelve (darse davāzdahom)

■ **(1) POLITE PHRASES & CONVENTIONS**

Persian has an enormous variety of polite phrases and expressions which, while they will sound very flowery in translation, especially to anyone accustomed to the more brief and basic politeness of western culture, are not just literary forms, but are in everyday use. Here are a few of them:

khêıli khoshvaghtam, or **khoshvaghtam** – I am very fortunate [to meet you]; *used on being introduced to someone*

The same expression can be used when saying goodbye after having being introduced for the first time:

khodāfez, khoshvaght shodam, or, **khêıli khoshvaght shodam**

marhamat ziād and **lotfetun ziād** ('may you have much favour', 'may you have much honour') are commonly used when saying goodbye, as is the expression **sāyeye shomā kam nashe** or **sāyatun kam nashe** which means 'may your shadow never grow less'. Also used is **ghorbāne shomā**, literally 'may I be sacrificed for you', and, between closer friends **ghorbāne to** or even **ghorbānat** (See reading passage for Lesson 9).

The more colloquial **ghorbunet** or **ghorbunetam**, are also used in the sense of 'be a dear and...' or just 'please': **dar-o beband, ghorbunetam** or **ghorbunetam, dar-o beband** – Shut the door, there's a dear *or* do shut the door please

daste shomā dard nakone, or **dastet dard nakone** *lit.* 'may your hand never ache' is a common way of expressing thanks for a service performed.

jāye shomā khāli – 'your place was empty' is very often used when reporting on something that was good or was enjoyed:
diruz raftim gardesh, jāye shomā khāli khêıli khosh gozasht – We went on an outing yesterday; we had a very good time (and therefore your place was empty – i.e. it would have been nice if you could have been there too)

The word **befarmāid** (Lesson 5, Phrases and Expressions) is used all the time. In situations where there is no specific answer to **befarmāid**, for example when someone is asking you to go through a door first by saying **befarmāid**, it is usual to demur and say **khāhesh mikonam, shomā befarmāid** or **na, khāhesh mikonam, shomā befarmāid**, at least once. Likewise at a party or in people's homes you may see people being offered things – fruit, sweets etc. and first they will say **na mersi** in answer to the **befarmāid**, then after several **befarmāid**'s and **khāhesh mikonam**'s, they will finally accept what is being offered. This kind of process is known as **tārof**. The less well people know each other or the more respect they wish to show, the greater the degree of **tārof**. The verb **tārof kardan** means 'to offer someone something', but only in the sense of food, drink, etc.

chashm (which is derived from **be ruye cheshm**, 'upon my eyes') means 'certainly', 'of course', 'yes, I will' in answer to a command or request:

be pedaretun salām beresunid – **chashm** – Give my regards to your father – Yes, of course (**salām resundan**: to send regards, *lit.* to convey greetings; *the same expression is also used for* 'give my love to')

arz kardan is a polite version of **goftan** ('to say'), usually used when referring to yourself, and **farmudan** ('to command') is used when referring to others: e.g. **arz kardam** – I said, **farmudid** – you said

tabrik arz mikonam	Congratulations; I congratulate you. *To be less formal one can say* **behetun tabrik migam** (*or* **behet tabrik migam**, *for the familiar*)
tasliat arz mikonam	Please accept my condolences; I offer my condolences. *Less formal:* **behet/ behetun tasliat migam**

At the New Year and on joyous religious festivals the greeting is: **êide shomā mobārak**

mobārak ('blessed') is also used to comment favourably on something new:
e.g.: **kafshe now pushidi?**
    āre
    mobārak (*or* **mobārak-e**, *or* **mobāraket bāshe**)
and **kāre jadid mobārak** – Congratulations on your new job

■ (2) OTHER EXPRESSIONS
(a)   The use of oaths to reinforce what is being said is quite common, so you get expressions like:

bekhodā (*short for* **be khodā ghassam** – I swear to God) –
By God, which means little more than 'honestly', 'truly'

vāllā, bevallāhe   –   *more or less like* **bekhodā**

vāllā is also used as an interjection, rather like 'well':
'**chi goft?**' '**vāllā, dorost nafahmidam vali mesle in ke goft
fardā miād**'. – 'What did he say?' 'Well, I didn't quite
understand, but I think he said he'd come tomorrow'.

be ghor'ān	–	By the Koran
be ghor'āne majid	–	By the glorious Koran: *these two expressions are slightly stronger than* **bekhodā** *and are obviously usually only used by Moslems.*

(*b*)   The following swear words may be heard, but it is clearly
not a good idea to use them!

gom sho, *or* **boro gom sho** – Get lost!
pedar sag – *lit.* your father's a dog; *very insulting since dogs
are unclean to Moslems*
pedar sukhté – *lit.* burnt father, i.e. he's in hell, or should
go there
khāk bar sar/saret – *lit.* earth on your head; drop dead

Situational Phrases and Conversations

■ AT THE AIRPORT

ghesmate gozarnāme	The passport section
salām	Greetings
khosh āmadid	Welcome
chand vaght mimunid?	How long are you staying?
do hafte	Two weeks
ādresetun dar Irān kojā-st?	What is your address in Iran?

mahale eghāmatetun dar Irān kojā-st?	Where are you staying in Iran?
hotel āzādi	The Azadi Hotel
befarmāid jelo	Move forward please
befarmāid intaraf	Come this way please
sālone gomrok	Customs hall
anjāme tashrifāte gomroki	*lit*: The carrying out of customs formalities, i.e. going through customs
chi dārin?	What have you got/Anything to declare?
hichi, faghat lavāzeme shakhsi	Nothing, only personal effects
sigār o mashrub ke nadārid?	You haven't any alcohol or cigarettes, have you?
cherā, sigār dāram vali mashrub nadaram	Yes I do, I have cigarettes but no alcohol
nakhêir	No I do not
lotfan in chameduno bāz konid	Please open this suitcase
befarmāid	Here you are
barāye in bāyad gomrok bedid	You must pay customs duty on this
arz chi darin?	What foreign currency have you got?
meghdāri dolār o pond	Some dollars and pounds
bāyad forme arz por konid	You must fill in a currency form
charkh dasti	Trolley
bār bar	Porter
bānde forudgāh	The runway
havāpêima ta'khir dāre	The plane is late
etelā'āt kojā-st?	Where is the information desk?
befarmāid tuye saf	Please join the queue
vorud	Entrance
khoruj	Exit
sālone entezār	Waiting room

■ AT THE TRAVEL AGENT

mikhām yek jā barāye Landan rezerv konam	I would like to make a reservation for London
besyār khob. barāye che ruzi?	Certainly. For what day?
shambe avvale ut	Saturday August the first
mota'asefāne un parvāz jā nadāre	Unfortunately there are no seats on that flight
agar bekhāhid barāye do shambash mitunam behetun jā bedam	If you like I can give you a seat for the Monday
ya'ni sevvome ut?	You mean August the third?
bale	Yes
bāshe, pas do shambe	Alright, Monday then
khêli khob barāye do shambe rezerv mikonam. agar ham bekhāhid mitunam tuye liste entezāre shambe ham shomā ro bezāram.	Very well, I'll make the booking for Monday. If you like I can also put you on the waiting list for the Saturday.
bale, bi zahmat in kār ro bokonid va agar jā bud beman khabar bedin.	Yes, please do so and let me know if there is a seat.
esmetun rā befarmāid	Your name, please
shomāreye telefonetun chand-e?	What is your telephone number?
bi zahmat in jāye mano ta'id konid	Could you please confirm my reservation.
otobuse Esfahān che sā'ati harekat mikone?	What time does the Esfahan bus leave?
sā'ate panje sob	At five a.m.
mitunam az hālā bilit bekharam?	Can I buy a ticket now?
bale albatte	Yes of course
terane Tabriz az kudum sakku harekat mikone?	Which platform does the Tabriz train leave from?
sakkuye panj	Platform five
che sā'ati vārede Tabriz mishe?	At what time does it reach Tabriz?

shishe sobe fardā	Six o'clock tomorrow morning
bilite turbo teran barāye Mashhad dārid?	Do you have any tickets for the turbo train to Mashad?
mota'asefāne tamām shodé.	I'm afraid there aren't any left
mitunid bā ghatāre sari'ol seîr berin.	You can take the express
besyār khob, pas yek bilite raft o bar gasht beman bedin	Alright, I'll have a return, please
darejeye yek mikhāid?	First class?
bale	Yes
befarmāid	Here you are
cheghadr mishe?	How much is it?
divist o panjā toman	Two hundred and fifty tomans

■ SHOPPING

salām āghā/khānum, befarmāid	Good morning, what can I do for you?
salām, shir darin?	Good morning. Is there any milk?
pākati tamām shodé ammā shishei hast	The cartons are finished but we have bottled milk
bāshe, pas bi zahmat yeki beman bedid	Alright then, could I have one please
befarmāid. chize dige ham lāzem dārid?	There you are. Anything else?
bale, ye ghāleb kare, divist o panjā geram panir o yek chāiye nim kilo'i	Yes, butter, two hundred and fifty grammes of cheese and a half kilo packet of tea
karash cheghadri bāshe?	What size butter do you want?
unam divist o panjā gerami bāshe khub-e	Two hundred and fifty grammes will be fine
befarmāid	Here you are
pākat dārin	Do you have a bag?
cheghadr shod?	How much is it?

navad o panj toman o panj ezar	Ninety-five tomans five rials
befarmāid	Here you are
mersi, āghā/khānum	Thank you sir/madam
khodāfez	Goodbye

in pārche metri chand-e?	How much a metre is this material?
shast o panj toman	Sixty-five tomans
khêili gerun-e arzuntaresh o nadārid	It's very expensive, haven't you got anything cheaper?
na, mota'assefāne tamum shodé	No, unfortunately it's all gone
takhfif ham nadāre?	Can't you give me a reduction?
aslan	No, I can't
khêilekhob, do metr bedin	Alright, give me two metres
befarmāid pulesh o bedin sandogh residesh o biārid jensetun o begirin	Pay at the cash desk, please. Bring the receipt and take your goods

portaghālā kiloi chand-e?	How much are the oranges per kilo?
punzda toman	Fifteen tomans
pas se kilo bedin	Give me three kilos, then

◀ ASKING THE WAY

bānke markazi az kudum taraf-e?	How does one get to the Central Bank?
sare avvalin chār rāh daste rāst bepichid, tuye hamun khiābun daste rāstetun-e	Turn right at the first crossroads. It is then in that road, on your right
bebakhshid, āghā/khānum, vezārate keshāvarzi kojā-st?	Excuse me, sir/madam, where is the Ministry of Agriculture?
ākhare hamin khiābun-e	It's at the end of this road
khêili dur-e?	Is it very far?

na, piāde ham mitunid berid	No, you can walk it if you want
daste chap bepichid	Turn left
mostaghim berid	Go straight on

■ THE TELEPHONE

allo	Hello
befarmāid	Yes?
manzele āghāye Haghighi?	Is that Mr Haghighi's residence?
nakhêir, eshtebāh-e	No, you've got the wrong number
bebakhshid	I'm sorry
allo	Hello
manzele āghāye Haghighi?	Is that Mr Haghighi's residence?
befarmāid	Yes
āghā tashrif dārand?	Is Mr Haghighi in?
bale, shomā?	Yes. Who's that speaking?
man John Smith	This is John Smith
gushi khedmatetun	Hold the line, please
salām āghāye Smith	Hello, Mr Smith
salām, hāle shomā chetowr-e?	Hello, how are you?
mersi, be marhematetun, bad nistam, befarmāid	I'm not too bad, thank you, what can I do for you?
vāllā, mikhāstam bebinam kêi vaght dārid biām shomā ro bebinam	Well, I wanted to ask when I could come and see you
khāhesh mikonam, har sā'ati ke befarmāid man hāzeram	Any time you say
seshambe chetowr-e?	What about Tuesday?
seshambe che sā'ati?	What time on Tuesday?
har sā'ati shomā bekhāid/ bekhāhid	Any time you say
sā'ate panj khub-e?	Is five o'clock alright?

bale, khêli khub-e	Yes, that's fine
besyār khob, pas sā'ate panj mibinametun. daftare man-o baladid?	Very well, then, I'll see you at five o'clock. Do you know where my office is?
bale	Yes
pas tā seshambe, khodāfez	Well, till Tuesday, then
khodāfez/khodā hāfeze shomā	Goodbye
marhemat ziād	Goodbye

IN A TAXI

tā Shemrun cheghadr migirid, āghā?	How much do you charge to go to Shemran?
bi zahmat berim mêidune Ferdowsi	(To) Ferdowsi Square, please
or: mêidune Ferdowsi, lotfan	

on reaching your destination:

cheghadr shod?	How much is it?

Appendix

NUMBERS

The Arabic numerals, which are also used in Persian, are as follows:

١	٢	٣	٤	٥	٦	٧	٨	٩	١٠
1	2	3	4	5	6	7	8	9	10

123 = ١٢٣   65 = ٦٥   2695 = ٢٦٩٥

The decimal point is represented by a comma.

CURRENCY

Notes and coins currently in circulation are:

COINS
1 rial (**yegheruni**)
2 rials (**dozāri**)
5 rials (**paynzāri**)
10 rials (**ye-tomani**)
20 rials (**do-tomani**)
50 rials (**panj-tomani**)

NOTES
100   rials (**da-tomani**)
200   rials (**bis-tomani**)
500   rials (**panjā-tomani**)
1000 rials (**sad-tomani**)
2000 rials (**divis-tomani**)
5000 rials (**punsad tomani**)
10000 rials (**hezār tomani**)

THE CALENDAR

In Iran, the Islamic months are called:

moharram
safar
rabi'ol avval
rabi'os-sāni
jamādi ol avval
jamādi os-sāni

rajab
sha'bān
ramazān
shavvāl
zigha'de
zihajje

The chief civil public holidays are:

(approximate corresponding date)

1 – 4 Farvardin	–	*Now Ruz* holidays	(21–24 March)
12 Farvardin	–	Islamic Republic Day	(1 April)
13 Farvardin	–	thirteenth of *Now Ruz*	(2 April)
15 K̲h̲ordād	–	Popular uprising of 1963	(5 June)
17 S̲h̲ahrivar	–	Commemoration of the martyrs of the revolution	(8 September)
22 Bahman	–	Islamic Revolution Day	(11 February)
29 Esfand	–	Nationalisation of the Oil Industry	(19 March)

The chief religious public holidays are:

13 rajab	–	Birthday of Ali, the Prophet's son-in-law
27 rajab	–	**êide mab'as**: the anniversary of the day Mohammad began his ministry
15 s̲h̲a'bān	–	Birthday of the 12th Imam
21 ramazān	–	The martyrdom of Ali
1 s̲h̲avvāl	–	*êide fetr*: the celebration of the ending of the fasting month of Ramadan
25 s̲h̲āvvāl	–	Death of Imam Ja'far Sāde̲g̲h̲
11 zigha'de	–	Birthday of Emam Rezā (the 8th Imam of the Shiites)
10 zihajje	–	*êide g̲h̲orbān*: the day on which pilgrims to Mecca make sacrifices
18 zihajje	–	*êide g̲h̲adir*: the anniversary of the day Ali was appointed successor to the Prophet
9 moharram	–	*tāsu'ā*: the eve of Imam Hussein's martyrdom

10 moharram	–	*āshurā*: martyrdom of Imam Hussein
20 safar	–	*arba'in*: 40th day of the martyrdom of Imam Hussein
28 safar	–	Death of the Prophet and martyrdom of Imam Hassan
17 rabi-ol avval	–	Birthday of the Prophet, birthday of Imam Ja'far Sādegh

Order to your bookseller or to…

ROUTLEDGE, CHAPMAN AND HALL INC.
29 West 35th Street
New York
NY 10001
USA

ROUTLEDGE
Associated Book Publishers
North Way
Andover, Hants.
SP10 5BE
ENGLAND

cassette. The pronunciation guide, readings, conversations and idiomatic phrases contained in the book have been recorded by native speakers of Persian, making the cassette an invaluable aid to speaking and comprehension.

If you have been unable to obtain the course pack the cassette can be ordered separately through your bookseller or, in case of difficulty, cash with order from Routledge Limited, Associated Book Publishers, North Way, Andover, Hants SP10 5BE, price £7.95 including V.A.T., or from Routledge, Chapman and Hall Inc. 29 West 35th Street, New York, N.Y. 10001, U.S.A.

For your convenience an order form is attached.

CASSETTE ORDER

Please supply one/two/ ..... cassette(s) of

Moshiri, *Colloquial Persian*

ISBN 0-415-00887-5

Price £7.95 inc V.A.T.

☐ I enclose payment with order.

☐ Please debit my Access/Mastercharge/Visa/American Express account number

Name

Address

Exercise Key

Lesson One

A. 1. ghazā khub-e 2. āb garm-e 3. panjere bāz nist 4. salām 5. hāle shomā chetowr-e? 6. khub-am, mersi 7. khodāfez 8. khunei; sandali; mardi; OR ye khune; ye sandali; ye mard 9. hotel kojā-st? 10. kudum hotel? hotel Esteghlāl 11. panj ketāb 12. nun tāz-ast 13. dokhtar kuchik-e 14. havā garm nist 15. khune bozorg nist 16. āb sard-e 17. mādar bad nist 18. pedarā; panjerehā; pesarā 19. pir o javun 20. otāgh tamiz-e?

B. 1. The bread isn't fresh 2. The weather is hot. 3. The weather is hot. 4. The boy is big. 5. Where's the table? 6. The door is open. 7. Is the window closed? 8. Which window? 9. The girl isn't naughty. 10. The grandmother is sick. 11. Flies are dirty. 12. What's the weather like?

Lesson Two

A. 1. khuneye man bozorgtar az khuneye Hasan-e 2. bozorgtarin khune ruye tappe ast 3. māshine man kuchiktar az māshine Hasan-e 4. lebāse Fāteme tamiztar az lebāse Maryam-e 5. in lebās az hame tamiztar-e 6. hotel tamiz-e 7. otāghe man kuchik-e OR otāgham kuchik-e 8. in ketābe to-st 9. un miz kasif-e 10. in chame-dune siāhe man-e

B. 1. Your ticket is on the table. 2. The big girl's dress is white. 3. Maryam's mother is ill. 4. This door is open. 5. That boy is naughty. 6. My brother is the best. 7. The cleanest hotel. 8. My suitcase is black. 9. Where is the bus stop? 10. Where is the best hotel in town?

C. 1. ketābam 2. ketābe bozorgam 3. khunat kuchik-e OR khuneye to kuchik-e 4. māshinesh bozorg-e 5. dare bāgh bāz-e 6. lebāse dokhtar tamiz-e 7. otāghe mādaram bozorg-e 8. māshine pedaret kuchik-e OR māshine pedare to kuchik-e 9. khuneye pedaram ruye tappe ast 10. khāhare Hasan mariz-e

D. 1. ketābe Hasan 2. <u>kh</u>uneye mard 3. <u>kh</u>āhare man 4. <u>kh</u>uneye man 5. barādare<u>sh</u> 6. hotele <u>kh</u>ub 7. bilite otobus 8. ye far<u>sh</u>e bozorg 9. ketābe <u>sh</u>omā 10. <u>ch</u>ar<u>kh</u>e mā<u>sh</u>in

Lesson Three

A. 1. My room was big and clean. 2. My friend came from the office. 3. Maryam had breakfast. 4. My friend's house wasn't far. 5. Are you English? 6. The bus was full. 7. The taxi was empty. 8. Hasan went to the office every day. 9. I sat and read the papers for a bit. 10. He went to the hotel with his friend. 11. Why did you come? 12. There was a gentle breeze blowing.

B. 1. havāpêimā dir resid 2. otāgham bozorg o tamiz bud 3. dustam unjā nabud 4. diruz nayāmadim 5. mon<u>sh</u>i nāme neminave<u>sh</u>t 6. nāme nanave<u>sh</u>ti? 7. madreseye do<u>kh</u>taret unjā-st 8. rafti <u>kh</u>una<u>sh</u>?

C. 1. havāpêimā dir naresid 2. otāgham bozorg o tamiz nabud 3. dustam unjā nabud 4. diruz nayāmadim 5. mon<u>sh</u>i nāme neminave<u>sh</u>t 6. nāme nanave<u>sh</u>ti? 7. madreseye do<u>kh</u>taret <u>un</u>jā nist 8. narafti <u>kh</u>una<u>sh</u>?

Lesson Four

A. 1. The weather is cold, it's snowing. 2. The secretary is writing a letter. 3. I'll go as soon as possible. 4. I want to go (on foot) and buy some fruit. 5. Mariam buys medicine for her son at the chemist's. 6. We eat bread and cheese and drink tea for breakfast. 7. My friend couldn't come with us. 8. I'll go to the office tomorrow. 9. Close the door.

B. 1. Hasan har ruz be edāre mire 2. har ruz unjā nemire 3. bārun miād? 4. ingilisi hastid? 5. na, irāni hastam, ingilisi nistam 6. mi<u>kh</u>ād biād <u>kh</u>unam 7. fardā miām 8. <u>ch</u>erā āmadid? 9. kojā mire? 10. fardā kojā miri?

C. 1. miram/miravam; miraftam; beram/beravam
   2. migim/miguim; migoftim; begim/beguim
   3. mirunid; mirundid; berunid
   4. mi<u>kh</u>orand; mi<u>kh</u>ordand; bo<u>kh</u>orand

5. mishe/mishavad; mishod; beshe/beshavad

D. 1. begu 2. beshno/besheno 3. bokhor 4. bodo 5. biā

Lesson Five

A. 1. The driver opened the door. 2. My son closed the door. 3. He brought the book. 4. He bought the bus ticket at the window. 5. The naughty boy falls down a lot. 6. I went to the hotel and had a bath. 7. It has got very cold and it rains every day. 8. I took off my clothes. 9. Open the door; don't go near the water; close the window. 10. I arrived late and the bus had left.

B. 1. dar o bast; chāi ro āvord; ghazā ro khord 2. ruznāme kharid; ye chāi khord; ghazā khordim 3. otobuse hotel o didand 4. moāvene vazir o didim 5. dustam dar o bāz kard, goft: biā tu 6. yek nafar sedā zad: negah dār 7. dar o bāz nakon 8. bi zahmat panjere ro beband 9. otobus rafté 10. tāksi āmadé?

Lesson Six

A. 1. My friend and I went to the cinema the day before yesterday. 2. Come tomorrow and we'll go shopping together. 3. Why did you come so late last night? 4. I waited for about twenty minutes but the bus didn't come. 5. My father hasn't come back from his travels yet. 6. Why didn't you go together? 7. My office is near the bazaar. 8. I'm going to university next year. 9. We went to Turkey by car last year. 10. The town bus/the bus to town passes our house mornings and evenings. 11. Have you seen my shoes? Yes, they're under your bed. 12. Tell me, was anyone else there apart from you?

B. 1. livān ruye miz bud 2. bachche āheste az pellehā bālā raft 3. kāram o diruz tamum kardam. 4. pārsāl raftim Pāris OR pārsāl be Pāris raftim 5. dustam khub mirune OR dustam khub rānandegi mikone 6. dokhtaram dir be khune āmad OR dokhtaram dir āmad khune 7. teran khêili tond mire 8. kifet o injā bezār OR kifetun o injā bezārid 9. bā chi umadi? 10. pārsāl bā havāpêimā raftand Landan

C. 1. bā 2. be 3. az 4. barāye 5. az 6. tuye 7. be

Lesson Seven

A. 1. A hundred and thirty-five people work in our office. 2. My mother bought two white dresses OR shirts. 3. How many children have you got? 4. Buy me three kilos of meat. 5. How many brothers and sisters has she got? 6. How many people were on the bus? 7. He gave me a third of his money. 8. I need five or six metres of material. 9. The cost of houses has gone up by twenty percent. 10. Where can I buy a good pair of shoes?

B. 1. chand sālet-e? chand sāletun-e? 2. chehel o panj sālam-e 3. pesaram chahār sālesh-e 4. nesfe nun o khord 5. Irān do reshte kuhe bozorg dāre 6. se dafe behesh telefon kardam 7. do dafe be edāreye man āmadé 8. vazir o yek bār didam OR vazir o ye dafe didam 9. in portaghālā kilo'i chand-e? 10. chand nafar tuye otāgh budand?

Lesson Eight

A. Mariam has one book. Hassan gave her two exercise books today. Mariam is going to go to school on Saturday. Mariam's school is big. It has about seven hundred pupils. There are about forty pupils in each class. In Iran the children only have Fridays off. Most schools' hours are from eight to half past one from Saturday to Wednesday. On Thursdays they only work till twelve. The academic year begins on the first of Mehr and usually goes straight through until towards the end of Khordad. They do also have thirteen days' Now Ruz holiday at the beginning of spring.

B. 1. shambe miād 2. sā'at haft o bist daigh-ast 3. sā'ate hasht jalese dāram 4. shish māhe dige emtahān dāram 5. māhe āyande barāye kār be Engelestān miram OR māhe dige barāye kār be Engelestān miram 6. sā'ate hafte sob bāyad forudgā bāsham 7. sā'ate hashte ba'd az zohre diruz barāye Landan harekat kardand OR sā'ate hashte ba'd az zohre diruz betarafe Landan harekat kardand 8. teran che sā'ati harekat mikone? 9. khāhesh mikonam dir nakon chun khêili kār dāram OR khāhesh mikonam dir nayā chun khêili kār dāram 10. hafteye pish har ruz kār kardam 11. pule khurd nadārid? 12. haftome ordibeheshte hezaro sisado shasto shish

Lesson Nine

A. 1. Don't use that pen, it's mine OR Don't take that pen, it's mine. 2. Most of this land belongs to the state. 3. Guess who I saw yesterday? 4. I knocked and knocked but nobody answered (*lit.* However much I knocked, nobody answered). 5. I studied all day yesterday. 6. Have you seen my black pen? 7. I want to go to the seaside for Now Ruz this year. They say the weather is very good there at that time of year. 8. This is very easy, why don't you do it yourself? 9. Didn't you know today was a holiday? (*lit.* Didn't you know everywhere was closed today?) 10. Don't ever do that, I really dislike it.

B. 1. hichkas unjā nabud 2. cherā khodet nemiri? cherā khodetun nemirid? 3. kife sefide man-o nadidi? OR kif sefidéye man-o nadidi? OR kif sefidàm-o nadidi? 4. un restorān ghazāsh khêili bad-e 5. māshinet-o chikār kardi? dorostesh kardam 6. un pusha ro var nadār, māle man-e 7. az hichkudum az in kafshā khosham nemiād OR hich kudum az in kafshā ro dust nadāram 8. tamāme shab tuye havāpêimā budam 9. ba'zi dokkunā fardā basté-and OR ba'zi maghāzehā fardā ta'til-and 10. bā māshine khodesh umad

Lesson Ten

A. 1. He asked me to come. 2. The passenger asked what time the plane would leave. 3. The child cried itself to sleep. 4. I can come and collect you and take you shopping if you want. 5. If you'd told me you didn't have a car I'd have come sooner. 6. Do you have room if I should want to stay an extra night? 7. I may not want to go out tomorrow. 8. He shut the window so hard that the glass broke. 9. If you work hard you'll progress fast. 10. If you'd come with us yesterday, you'd have enjoyed yourself.

B. 1. beman goft ke tamāme ruz khune mimune 2. goft ke sa'y mikone kife pulam-o pêidā kone 3. azam porsid ke chikār mikhām bokonam 4. fekr kardam diruz miāi 5. agar midunestam in ketāb-o dāri nemikharidamesh 6. agar umad behesh bogu ke man raftam 7. momkene beman begid davākhune kojā-st? 8. agar fardā biām hāzer-e? 9. fekr nakonam dorost beshe OR fekr nemikonam dorost beshe 10. agar sabr konam mitunam doktor-o bebinam?

Lesson Eleven

A. 1. He succeeded by being clever/hardworking *OR* He succeeded through cleverness/hard work. 2. He was dying of hunger and thirst. 3. You ought not to go out (in the street) without Islamic dress. 4. If you miss the train I'll take you there in the car. 5. There are many cities worth seeing in Europe. 6. The new singer's voice is really worth hearing. 7. In the end I don't know whether this can be done or not. 8. I went to collect my watch yesterday and the man said it wasn't ready. 9. The driver didn't see the red light and hit another car. 10. That girl was very cheeky.

B. 1. az khastegi dāram mimiram 2. bā tambali kāret pish nemire/ nakhāhad raft 3. Shirāz zibā va didani-st 4. mikhāstam dare khunam-o avaz konam vali marde goft ke shodani nist 5. dustam goft ke man-o miresune 6. pesarak kheîli khaste bud 7. pesare behem zabun derāzi kard 8. teflak kheîli khaste shodé bud

C. badi; tambali; bad bakhti

English–Persian Glossary

abbreviation: k̲h̲olāse
ability: este'dād
able: bā este'dād, tavānā; **to be able**, tavānestan (tavān)
about: (*concerning*) dar bāreye; (*nearly*) tag̲h̲riban; (*to be about to*) mik̲h̲āst . . .
above: bālāye
abroad: k̲h̲ārej
absent: g̲h̲āyeb
absent-minded: havās part
absolute: motlag̲h̲, g̲h̲at'i
absolutely: be kolli, kāmelan
absurd: bima'ni, mozak̲h̲raf
abuse *vb*: (*verbally*) fohsh dādan (deh)
accept: g̲h̲abul kardan (kon)
accident: pishāmad, ettefāg̲h̲, tasādof; (*mistake*) eshtebāh; **to have an accident**, tasādof kardan (kon)
accidentally: (*by chance*) ettefāg̲h̲an, tasādofan; (*by mistake*) eshtebāhan
accommodation: **to have accommodation**, jā dāshtan (dār)
according to: motābeg̲h̲e
account: hesāb; (*description*) sharh
accountant: hesābdār
accurate: dag̲h̲ig̲h̲
accustomed: **to get accustomed**, ādat kardan (kon)
ace: ās, takk̲h̲āl
acquaintance: āshnā; **to be acquainted**, āshnā budan (bāsh)
across: **to go across**, obur kardan (kon), rad shodan (shav)
act *vb*: amal kardan (kon); (*in a play*) bāzi kardan (kon)
action: amal, eg̲h̲dām
active: fa'āl
actor: honar pishe
add: jam' kardan (kon)
addicted: mo'tād
addition: jam'
additional: ezāfi

address *n*: ādres, ne<u>sh</u>āni
adjust: tanzim kardan (kon)
administration: edāre
advertisement: āgahi, e'lān
advice: nasihat, towsiye
affection: mohabbat, alā<u>gh</u>e
afraid: to be afraid, tarsidan (tars)
after: ba'd (az)
afternoon: ba'd az zohr; (*late afternoon*) asr
afterwards: ba'dan
again: do bāre
against: zedde, bar zedde, mo<u>kh</u>ālefe
age *n*: sen
agency: namāyandegi, ā<u>zh</u>āns
agree: movāfe<u>gh</u>at kardan (kon)
agreement: movāfe<u>gh</u>at
agriculture: ke<u>sh</u>āvarzi
air: havā; **air mail**, poste havā'i
air-conditioning: tahviye; (*cooler*) kuler
air force: niruye havāi
aircraft: havāpêımā
airport: forudgāh
alarm *n*: zange <u>kh</u>atar, ā<u>zh</u>ir
algebra: jabr
alike: <u>sh</u>abih
alive: zende
all: hame
allow: ejāze dādan (deh)
almond: bādām
alone: tanhā
along: (*along the length of*) dar tule; (*beside*) dar kenāre
alphabet: alefbā
also: ham<u>ch</u>enin
although: bā vojudike, bā vojude inke, gar<u>ch</u>e
always: hami<u>sh</u>e
ambassador: safir; safir kabir
ambulance: āmbulāns
America: āmrikā
American: āmrikā'i

among: bêine
amount: meghdār; (*of money*) mablagh
ancient: ghadimi; (*history, architecture*) bāstāni
and: va, o
angel: fereshte
angry: asabāni
animal: hêivān
ankle: moche pā
announce: e'lān kardan (kon), khabar dādan (deh)
annual: sālāne
another: digar
answer *n*: javāb
ant: murche
anti-aircraft gun: (tupe) zedde havāi
antique: atighe
anxious: negarān, delvāpas
any: har
anyhow: behar hāl
anyone: har kas
anything: har chiz
apartment: āpārtemān
apologize: ma'zerat khāstan (khāh)
appetite: eshtehā
apple: sib
applicant: darkhāst konande, dāvtalab, motaghāzi
application form: darkhāst, form
approach *vb*: nazdik shodan (shav)
appropriate: monāseb
approximate: taghribi
apricot: zardālu
Arab: arab
Arabic: arabi
architect: me'mār; ārshitekt
area: masāhat
argue: da'vā kardan (kon), bahs kardan (kon)
arithmetic: hesāb
arm: bāzu (*also* dast)
Armenian: armani
arms: (*weapons*) aslahe, selāh

army: arte<u>sh</u>
around: dowre
arrange: tartib dādan (deh), <u>ch</u>idan (<u>ch</u>in)
arrest *vb*: bāzdā<u>sh</u>t kardan (kon), tow<u>gh</u>if kardan (kon)
arrival: vorud (*entrance*); residan
arrive: residan (res)
art: honar
article:(*literary*) ma<u>gh</u>āle
artificial: masnu'i
artillery: tup<u>kh</u>āne
as: (*like*) mesle; (*because*) <u>ch</u>un; **as long as**, tā; **as soon as**,
  haminke, tā; **as soon as possible**, har <u>ch</u>e zudtar
ashamed: <u>kh</u>ejel, <u>sh</u>armande; **to be ashamed** <u>kh</u>ejālat ke<u>sh</u>idan
  (ke<u>sh</u>)
ashes: <u>kh</u>ākestar
ashtray: zir sigāri
Asia: asyā
ask: (*a question*) porsidan (pors), so'āl kardan (kon); **to ask for**,
  <u>kh</u>āstan (<u>kh</u>ah)
ass: <u>kh</u>ar, olā<u>gh</u>
assistant: dastyār, <u>sh</u>āgerd, komak; (*deputy*) mo'āven
aspirin: āspirin
at: dar
athlete: varze<u>sh</u>kār
atmosphere: jav, havā
attaché: vābaste
attack: *n* hamle; *vb* hamle kardan (kon)
attempt *vb*: sa'y kardan (kon), ku<u>sh</u>idan (ku<u>sh</u>)
attend: hāzer budan (bā<u>sh</u>)
attention: tavajjoh
attractive: jazzāb
aunt: (*paternal*) amme; (*maternal*) <u>kh</u>āle
author: (*writer*) nevisande
automatic: otomātik, <u>kh</u>odkār
autumn: pā'iz
avalanche: bahman
avenue: <u>kh</u>iābān
average: motavasset, miyāngin; (*normal*) āddi
awake: bidār

axe: tabar
axle: mile, mehvarcharkh

back: posht
backbone: sotune fagharāt
backgammon: takhtenard, takhte, shish o besh
bad: bad
bag: kif
baker: nānvā
balcony: bālkon, êivān
ball: tup
balloon: bād konak
banana: mowz
bank: bānk
banknote: eskenās
bankrupt: varshekasté
barber: salmāni
bare: lokht; berehne
barefoot: pā berehne
bargain *vb*: chune zadan (zan)
barley: jow
barracks: pādegān
base: pāye; (*military*) pāyegāh
basic: asāsi
basin: kāse
basket: sabad
bat: shab kur
bath: hammām
bathroom: hammām
battle: jang, nabard
battle-front: jebhe
battle-field: mêidāne jang
bazaar: bāzār
be: budan (bāsh)
beach: sāhel; plāzh
bead: mohre
bean: lubiā; **broad bean**, bāghāli; **kidney bean**, lubiā ghermez;
   French bean, lubiā sabz
bear: khers
beard: rish

beautiful: zibā
because: barāye inke
become: s̲h̲odan
bed: tak̲h̲te k̲h̲āb
bedding: rak̲h̲te k̲h̲āb
bedroom: otāg̲h̲e k̲h̲āb
bee: zanbur
beef: gus̲h̲te gāv
bee-hive: kandu
beer: ābejow
beetle: susk
beetroot: (*raw*) c̲h̲og̲h̲ondar; (*cooked*) labu
before: g̲h̲abl az; pis̲h̲ az
beg: gedā'i kardan (kon)
beggar: gedā
begin: s̲h̲oru' kardan (kon)
behalf: on behalf of, az tarafe
behaviour: raftār
behind: pos̲h̲te
believe: bāvar kardan (kon)
bell: zang
belong: māle (kasi yā c̲h̲izi) budan (bās̲h̲); (*more formal*) ta'llog̲h̲
   dās̲h̲tan (dār)
below: pā'ine, zire
belt: kamar band
bench: nimkat
bend *vb*: (*intrans.*) k̲h̲ām s̲h̲odan (s̲h̲av); (*trans.*) k̲h̲am kardan
   (kon)
benefit *vb*: manfa'at kardan (kon), sud bordan (bar)
beside: (*next to*) kenāre
between: bêine
bible: enjil
bicycle: doc̲h̲ark̲h̲e
big: bozorg
bill: (*invoice*) surat-hesāb (hesāb *for short*)
bird: parande
birth: tavallod; **to give birth**, zāidan (zā)
bite *vb*: gāz gereftan (gir); (*of insects*) nis̲h̲ zadan (zan), zadan
bitter: talk̲h̲

black: siāh, meshki
blanket: patu
bleed (*intrans. vb*): khun āmadan (ā)
blind *adj*: kur
blister *n*: toval
blood: khun
blossom *n*: shokufe
blouse: buluz, pirāhan (*coll*. pirhan)
blow: *n* zarbe; *vb* fut kardan (kon); (*of wind*) vazidan (vaz)
blue: ābi
blunt *adj*: kond
board *n*: takhte
boat: ghāyegh
body: badan, tan
boil *vb*: jushidan (jush)
bomb: *n* bomb; *vb*: bombārān kardan
bone: ostekhān (*coll*. ostokhun)
book: *n* ketāb; *vb* reserv kardan, jā gereftan (gir)
book-keeper: hesābdār
book-shop: ketābforushi
boot(s): chakme
border: *n* hāshie; (*of countries etc*) marz
bored: **I am bored**, howselam sar rafté
borrow: gharz kardan (kon)
both: har do
bottle: shishe, botri
bottom: tah; kaf
bowl: kāse
box: ja'be
boy: pesar
bracelet: dastband
brain: (*lit*.) maghz; (*fig*.) hush
brake *n*: tormoz
branch: (*of a tree*) shākhe; (*of a business, etc*) sho'be
brass: berenj
brave: shojā'
bread: nān
break *vb*: shekastan (shekan)
breakfast: sobhāne

breast: sine
breath: nafas
breathe: nafas keshidan (kesh)
bribe: *n* roshve; *vb* roshve dādan (deh)
brick: ājor
bride: arus
bridegroom: dāmād
bridge: pol
briefcase: kif
bright: rowshan, nurāni; (*clever*) bāhush
brim: labe
bring: āvardan (ār)
broadcast *vb*: pakhsh kardan (kon)
brooch: sanjāgh sine
broom: jāru
brother: barādar
brother-in-law: (*one's wife's brother*) barādar zan; (*one's husband's brother*) barādar showhar
bucket: satl
bud *n*: ghonche
budget *n*: budje
build: sākhtan (sāz)
building: sākhtemān, emārat
bulb: (*light*) lāmp; (*of flowers*) piāz
bullet: golule, tir
bunch: daste
burn *vb*: (*intrans.*) sukhtan (suz); (*trans.*) suzāndan (suzān)
bush: botte
business: (*occupation*) shoghl
busy: mashghul
but: ammā, vali
butcher: ghassāb
butter: kare
butterfly: parvāne
button: dogme
buy: kharidan (khar)
buyer: kharidār
by: kenāre; (*by means of transport*) bā; **by now**, tā hālā; **by the door**, kenāre dar; **by car**, bā māshin

cabbage: kalam
cabinet: (*govt.*) kābine
café: kāfe
cage: ghafas
calculate: hesāb kardan
calculator: mashine hesāb, mashinhesāb
calendar: taghvim
calf: (*animal*) gusāle
call *vb*: sedā kardan (kon), sedā zadan (zan)
calm: ārām
camel: shotor
camera: durbine akkāsi, durbin
cancel: bātel kardan
cancer: saratān
candle: sham'
cannon: tup
capital: (*of a country*) pāyetakht; (*financial*) sarmāye
capitalist: sarmāyedār
captain: (*army, police*) sarvān; (*of a ship*) nākhodā
car: māshin, otomobil
card: (*for playing*) varagh; (*business*) kārt; (*greetings card*) kārte tabrik
cardigan: kot, zhāket
careful: to be careful, movāzeb budan (bāsh); ehtiāt kardan (kon)
careless: bi ehtiāt
cargo: bār
carnation: mikhak
car park: pārking
carpenter: najjār
carpet: farsh, ghāli
carrots: havij
carry: haml kardan (kon)
case: (*box*) sandogh, ja'be; **in any case**, dar har surat; **in case**, agar
cash: naghd; pule naghd
cashier: sandoghdār
Caspian Sea: bahre khezer, daryāye khezer, daryāye māzandarān
cat: gorbe
catch *vb*: gereftan (gir)

cauliflower: gole kalam
caution: ehtiāt
caviare: khāviār
ceiling: saghf
celebration: jashn
celery: karafs
cellar: zir zamin
cement: simān
cemetery: ghabrestān, gurestān
central: markazi
century: gharn
chain *n*: zanjir
chair: sandali
chalk: gach
chance: (*accident*) ettefāgh, tasādof; (*opportunity*) forsat; **by chance**, ettefāghan
change: *n* taghyir, tabdil; (*money*) pule khurd; *vb* (*trans.*) avaz kardan (kon); (*intrans.*) avaz shodan (shav); **to change money**, pul khurd kardan (kon)
charcoal: zoghāl
chargé d'affaires: kārdār
charity: khêirāt; (*organization*) khêirieh
cheap: arzān
cheeky: por ru
cheese: panir
chemist: (*person*) dārusāz; (*shop*) davākhāne
chemistry: shimi
cheque: chek
cherry: gilās; ālbālu (*a particular kind of sour cherry*)
chess: shatranj
chest: (*box*) sandogh; (*breast*) sine
chew: javidan (jav) (*coll.* jowidan)
chicken: juje; morgh (*literally = hen, but usually used to refer to eating chicken where the very young bird is not specifically intended*)
chick-pea: nokhod
child: bachche
chimney: dud-kesh
chin: chane (*coll.* chune)

China: chin
china: (*porcelain*) chini
Chinese: chini
choose: entekhāb kardan (kon)
Christ: isā; (*messiah*) masih; isāye masih
Christian: masihi; isavi
church: kelisā
cigarette: sigār
cinema: sinemā
circle: dāyere
city: shahr
civilization: tamaddon
clean *adj*: tamiz, pāk
clear: sāf
clever: bā hush, zerang
climate: āb o havā
clock: sā'at
clock hand: aghrabeye sā'at
close *adj*: nazdik
close *vb*: bastan (band)
cloth: pārche
clothes: lebās
cloud: abr
coast: sāhel
coat: pālto
cock: khorus
coffee: ghahve
coin: sekke
cold: *adj* sard; *n* (*the common cold*) sarmā khordegi; **I have a cold**, sarmā khordéam (*coll.* sarmā khordam)
collar: yaghe
colleague: hamkār
collect: jam' kardan
college: dāneshkade
colour: rang
comb *n*: shāne (*coll.* shune)
come: āmādan (ā); **to come in**, tu āmādan
comfortable: rāhat
commerce: bāzargāni, tejārat

committee: komite
common: (*general*) omumi; (*usual*) āddi; (*joint*) mo<u>sh</u>tarek
company: <u>sh</u>erkat
compare: mog<u>h</u>āyese kardan (kon)
compel: majbur kardan (kon); vā dār kardan (kon)
competition: mosābeg<u>h</u>e
complain: <u>sh</u>ekāyat kardan (kon)
complete: kāmel
computer: komputer
condemn: mahkum kardan (kon)
condition: (*state*) vaz', hāl; (*stipulation*) <u>sh</u>art; (*state of affairs*) owzā'
confectioner: <u>gh</u>annādi
confess: e'terāf kardan (kon)
congratulate: tabrik goftan (gu)
connect: vasl kardan (kon), rabt dādan (deh)
conscience: vojdān
conscription: nezām vazife
constant: sābet, paydār
constipation: yobusat
consul: <u>gh</u>onsul
consult: ma<u>sh</u>verat kardan (kon)
contented: rāzi
continent: <u>gh</u>ārre
continue: edāme dādan (deh)
contract *n*: <u>gh</u>arārdād, peymān
contractor: peymānkar, mog<u>h</u>āte'ekar
control *n*: kontrol
conversation: sohbat
cook *n*: ā<u>sh</u>paz
cool *adj*: <u>kh</u>onak
cooler: kuler
co-operate: hamkāri kardan (kon)
copper: mes
copy *n*: runeve<u>sh</u>t
corn: gandom
corner: gu<u>sh</u>e
correct *adj*: sahih
correspondence: mokātebe

cost *n*: ghêimat, bahā
cotton: nakh
cotton-wool: pambe
cough *n*: sorfe
council: showrā
count *vb*: shemordan (shemor)
country: keshvar, mamlekat
coupon: kupon
courage: jor'at, daliri
courtyard: hayāt; (*in a mosque*) sahn
cousin: (*daughter of paternal aunt*) dokhtar ammeh; (*son of paternal aunt*) pesar ammeh; (*daughter/son of paternal uncle*) dokhtar/pesar amu; (*daughter/son of maternal aunt*) dokhtar/pesar khāle; (*daughter/son of maternal uncle*) dokhtar/pesar dāi
cow: madde gāv, gāv
crack: *n* tarak; *vb* tarak khordan (khor)
cream: khāme, sarshir
credit: e'tebār
creditor: talabkār
crime: jenāyat
criticism: enteghād
crooked: kaj
cross: *n* zarbdar; (*crucifix*) salib; *adj* (*angry*) asabāni; **he is cross**, oghātesh talkhe; *vb* obur kardan (kon), rad shodan (shav)
crossroads: chahār rāh
crowd: jam'iyyat
cry *vb*: (*weep*) gerye kardan (kon); (*shout*) dād zadan, faryād zadan (zan)
cucumber: khiār
cul-de-sac: bombast
culture: farhang
cup: fenjān
cupboard: ganje
cure *n*: darmān
curtain: parde
cushion: kusan; (*to lean against*) poshti; (*pillow*) bālesh
custom: rasm
customs: gomrok

cut *vb*: boridan (bor)

daily: ruzāne; (*in the sense of everyday*) ruzmarre
dairy products: labaniāt
dam: sadd
damage *n*: āsib, khesārat
damp: namnāk
dance: *n* raghs; *vb* raghsidan (raghs)
danger: khatar
dangerous: khatarnāk
dare: jor'at kardan (kon)
dark: tārik
date: (*time*) tārikh; (*fruit*) khormā
daughter: dokhtar
daughter-in-law: arus
dawn: sahar; (*less coll.*) bāmdād
day: ruz
dead: morde
dear: (*person etc*) aziz
death: marg
debt: bedehi, gharz
decide: tasmim gereftan (gir)
deduct: kam kardan (kon)
deep: amigh
defeat *n*: shekast
defect *n*: êib
definite: (*clear*) rowshan; (*final*) ghat'i, nahā'i
degree: dareje
delay *n*: ta'khir
delegate: namāyande
deliberately: amdan, makhsusan
delicate: zarif
deliver: tahvil dādan (deh)
demand *n*: khāstan
deny: enkār kardan (kon)
department: ghesmat, dāyere
depth: omgh, gowdi
desert: sahrā
desk: miztahrir
detective: kār āgāh

develop: (*film*) zāher kardan (kon)
devil: sheîtān
dew: shabnam
diameter: ghotr
diamond: almās; (*expensive, used in jewellery*) bereliān
diarrhoea: eshāl
dictionary: loghatnāme, diksioner
die: mordan
difference: fargh, tafāvot
difficult: sakht, moshkel
dig: kandan (kan)
digest: hazm kardan (kon)
dinner: (*evening meal*) shām
dining room: (otāghe) nāhārkhori
diploma: diplom
diplomat: diplomāt
direct *adv*: mostaghim
direction: jahat
director: modir
dirt: kesāfat
dirty: kasif
disconnect: ghat' kardan (kon)
discover: kashf kardan (kon)
discuss: bahs kardan (kon)
dish: zarf
dishwasher: māshine zarfshu'i
disinfect: zedde ofuni kardan (kon)
disrespect: bi-ehterāmi
dissolve: (*trans.*) hal kardan (kon); (*intrans.*) hal shodan (shav)
distance: fāsele
distinguish: tashkhis dādan (deh); (*recognise*) shenākhtan (shenās)
distribute: pakhsh kardan (kon)
district: mahalle; nāhiyye
dive *vb*: shirje raftan (rav)
divide: taghsim kardan (kon); ghesmat kardan (kon)
divorce *n*: talāgh
dizziness: sar gije
do: kardan (kon)
doctor: doktor, tabib, pezeshk

document: madrak (*pl.* madārek), sanad (*pl.* asnād)
dog: sag
doll: arusak
dome: gombad
donkey: olāgh, khar
door: dar
doubt: shak
dough: khamir
down: pā'in
drain: (*in sinks etc*) fāzel ab; (*general*) rāh ab; (*guttering*) nowdān
draw: (*picture*) naghghāshi kardan (kon); (*to pull*) keshidan (kesh)
drawer: kesho
dream: *n* khāb, rowyā; *vb* khāb didan (bin)
dress: pirhan; (*garment, also attire*) lebās
dressmaker: khayyāt
drink: *vb* nushidan; *n* (*non-alcoholic*) nushābe; (*alcoholic*) mashrub
drip *vb*: chekke kardan (kon)
drive *vb*: rāndan (rān); rānandegi kardan (kon)
drop: *vb* andākhtan (andāz); *n*: ghatre
drug: (*medicine*) davā, dāru; (*addictive drugs*) mavādde mokhadder
drunk: mast
dry: khoshk
duck: ordak, morghābi
dumb: lāl
dusk: ghorub
dust: gard, khāk, gard o khāk
dustman: supur
Dutch: holandi
duty: vazife; (*customs duty*) gomrok

each: har; **each one**, har yek
eagle: oghāb
ear: gush
early: zud
ear-ring: gushvāre
earth: zamin; (*soil*) khāk

earthquake: zelzele, zaminlarze
east: mashregh
easy: āsān
eat: khordan (khor)
economy: eghtesād
edge: labe
effect: asar
egg: tokhme morgh
egg-plant: bādemjān
Egypt: mesr
eight: hasht
eighteen: hijdah
eighty: hashtād
elastic: kesh
elect: entekhāb kardan (kon)
elections: entekhābāt
electricity: bargh
elementary: ebtedāi
elephant: fil
eleven: yāzdah
embassy: sefārat
embrace *vb*: baghal kardan (kon); (*to kiss*) busidan (bus)
emerald: zomorrod
emotions: ehsāsāt
employ: estekhdām kardan (kon)
empty: khāli
enamel: *n* lā'āb; *adj* lā'ābi
encourage: tashvigh kardan (kon)
end *n*: pāyān
enemy: doshman
engineer: mohandes
engine: motor
England: engelestān
English: ingilisi
enough: kāfi; bas
enter: vāred shodan (shav); dākhel shodan (shav)
entrance: vorud; (*fee*) vorudi
envelope: pākat
equal: mosāvi

error: eshtebāh
escape *n*: farār
especially: makhsusan
Europe: urupā
eve: shab
even: *prep* hattā; *adj* (*of numbers*) joft; (*level*) sāf; (*equal*) mosāvi;
  even if, valo inke
evening: asr, sare shab, shab
every: har
everyone: hame; hame kas
everywhere: hame jā
exact: daghigh, sahih
examination: emtehān; (*medical*) mo'āyene
example: mesāl
excellent: āli
except: joz; bejoz
exchange *vb*: avaz kardan (kon)
excitement: hayajān
excuse *vb*: bakhshidan
execution: e'dām
exempt *adj*: mo'āf
exercise *n*: (*sport*) varzesh; (*practice*) tamrin
exit: khoruj
expect: entezār dāshtan (dār)
expensive: gerān (*coll.* gerun)
experience: tajrobe
expert: khebre, motekhasses, kārshenās
explain: towzih dādan
explosion: enfejār
export *vb*: sāder kardan (kon); **exports**, sāderāt
extra: ezāfi
eye: cheshm

face: surat, ru
factory: karkhāne
faint *vb*: ghash kardan (kon)
fair: *adj* (*equitable*) ādelāne; (*hair*) bur
faith: imān
fall *vb*: oftādan (oft)

fame: shohrat
familiar: āshnā
family: khānevāde; fāmil
famous: ma'ruf; mashhur
fan: bād bezan; panke
far: dur
fare: kerāye
farmer: keshāvarz
fast: *adj* tond; sari'; *vb* ruze gereftan (gir)
fat: *adj* chāgh; *n* charbi
father: pedar
father-in-law: (*wife's father*) pedar zan; (*husband's father*) pedar
  showhar
fault: taghsir
fear: tars
feast day: êid
feather: par
fee: ojrat, mozd
feet: pā, pāhā
feel: hes kardan (kon); ehsās kardan (kon)
fellow countryman: hamvatan
fellow townsman: hamshahri
fellow traveller: hamsafar
festival: jashn
fever: tab
few: kam, andak; (*some*) chand, chandi, ba'zi
field: mazra'e
fifteen: pānzdah
fifty: panjāh
fig: anjir
fight *vb*: jangidan (jang)
figure: shekl, surat; (*body*) hêikal
file: sohān; (*of papers etc.*) parvande
finally: belakhare
find *vb*: pêidā kardan (kon)
fine *n*: jarime
finger: angosht
finish *vb*: tamām kardan (kon)
fir: kāj

fire: āte<u>sh</u>; **to catch fire**, āte<u>sh</u> gereftan (gir); **to set fire to**, āte<u>sh</u> zadan (zan)

fire-brigade: āte<u>sh</u> ne<u>sh</u>āni

first: avval

fish *n*: māhi

fist: mo<u>sh</u>t

fitted carpet: moket

five: panj

fix: dorost kardan (kon)

flag: par<u>ch</u>am, bêîra<u>gh</u>

flame: <u>sh</u>o'le

flat: sāf; (*apartment*) āpārteman

flea: kak

flood: seyl

floor: zamin; kaf

flour: ārd

flower: gol

fly: *n* magas; *vb* parvāz kardan (kon)

fog: meh

fold *vb*: tā kardan (kon)

follow: donbāl kardan (kon)

food: <u>gh</u>azā

fool: ahma<u>gh</u>

foot: pā; **to go on foot**, piāde raftan (rav)

football: futbāl

for: barāye

forbid: man' kardan (kon); <u>gh</u>ade<u>gh</u>an kardan (kon)

force *n*: zur

fore-arm: bāzu

forehead: pishāni

foreign: <u>kh</u>āreji

foreigner: <u>kh</u>āreji

forest: jangal

forget: farāmu<u>sh</u> kardan (kon)

forgive: ba<u>kh</u><u>sh</u>idan (ba<u>kh</u>sh)

fork: <u>ch</u>angāl

forty: <u>ch</u>ehel

forward: jelo, pi<u>sh</u>

fountain: favvāre

four: chahār
fourteen: chahārdah
fox: rubāh
fracture: shekastegi
frame: ghāb
France: farānse
free *adj*: āzād
freedom: āzādi
freeze: yakh zadan (zan)
freezer: frizer
freight: bār
French: farānsavi
fresh: tāze
Friday: jom'e
fridge: yakhchāl
friend: dust
frighten: tarsāndan (tarsān); **to be frightened**, tarsidan (tars)
frog: ghurbāghe
from: az
front: jelo, pish; (*battle-front*) jebhe; **in front of**, jeloye
frown: *n* akhm; *vb* akhm kardan (kon)
fruit: mive
fruiterer, fruitseller: miveforush
fry: sorkh kardan (kon)
frying pan: māhitāve, tāve
full: por
funny: mozhek; bā mazze; khandedār
furniture: mobl, asāse khāne
future *n*: āyande

game: bāzi
gaol: zendān
garage: gārāzh
garden: bāgh; bāghche
garlic: sir
gas: gāz
gas stove: ojāgh gāz, fere gāz
gate: darvāze
gear: (*of cars, etc.*) dande

gentleman: āghā
geography: joghrāfiā
German: ālmāni
Germany: ālmān
get: gereftan (gir)
gift: hedye, kādo
girl: dokhtar
give: dādan (deh)
glass: shishe; (*for drinking*) livān, gilās
glasses: (*spectacles*) êınak
glove: dastkesh
glue: chasb
go: raftan (rav)
goat: boz
God: khodā; (*Arabic*) allāh
goal: hadaf; (*in games*) gol
gold: talā
good: khub
goodbye: khodā hāfez
goods: ajnās
govern: hokumat kardan (kon)
government: dowlat, hokumat
gradually: tadrijan
grandchild: nave
grandfather: pedarbozorg
grandmother: mādarbozorg
grape: angur
grass: alaf; (*lawn*) chaman
grave *n*: ghabr, gur
graveyard: ghabrestān, gurestān
grease: *n* (*fat*) charbi; (*oil*) rowghan; *vb* charb kardan (kon);
   rowghan zadan (zan)
great: bozorg
Greece: yunān
greed: tama'
Greek: yunāni
green: sabz
greengrocer: sabzi forush
greet: salām kardan (kon)

grief: gham, ghosse, anduh
grocer: baghghāl
ground: zamin
group: daste, goruh
grow: roshd kardan (kon)
grumble: ghor zadan (zan)
guarantee *n*: zemānat
guess *vb*: hads zadan (zan)
guest: mehmān
guide *n*: rāhnamā
gulf: (*geographical*) khalij
gun: tofang; (*pistol*) haftir

hail: tagarg
hair: mu, zolf
half: nesf
hall: tālār; (*of a house*) hāl
halve: nesf kardan (kon)
hammer *n*: chakkosh
hand: dast
handkerchief: dastmāl
handle: daste
handsome: khoshkel
hang: (*trans.*) āvizān kardan (kon); (*intrans.*) āvizān shodan (shav); (*to execute*) dār zadan (zan)
happen: ettefāgh oftādan (oft)
happy: khoshhāl, shād
hard: (*firm*) seft; (*difficult*) sakht, moshkel
hare: khargush
harm: āsib
harvest *n*: mahsul
hat: kolāh
hate *vb*: tanaffor dāshtan (dār); motenaffer budan (bāsh)
have: dāshtan (dār)
hazel-nut: fandogh
he: u
head: sar
headache: sar dard
health: salāmati, tandorosti

hear: <u>sh</u>enidan (<u>sh</u>enav)
hearing aid: sam'ak
heart: <u>gh</u>alb
heat *n*: garmā
heaven: behe<u>sh</u>t
heavy: sangin
heel: pā<u>sh</u>ne
height: bolandi, ertefā'; (*of people*) <u>gh</u>add
hell: jahannam, duza<u>kh</u>
help *n*: komak
hen: mor<u>gh</u>
here: injā
hiccup *n*: sekseke
hide: (*trans.*) <u>gh</u>āyem kardan (kon); (*intrans.*) <u>gh</u>āyem <u>sh</u>odan (<u>sh</u>av)
high: boland, mortafa'
highway: bozorg rāh; <u>sh</u>āh rāh
hill: tappe
hinge: lowlā
hip: bāsan
hire *vb*: kerāye kardan (kon)
history: tāri<u>kh</u>
hit *vb*: zadan (zan)
hold *vb*: dar dast dā<u>sh</u>tan (dār); negah dā<u>sh</u>tan (dār)
hole: surā<u>kh</u>
holiday: ta'til; **holidays**, ta'tilāt
Holland: holand
hollow: puk, tu <u>kh</u>āli
home: manzel, <u>kh</u>āne
honest: dorost, dorostkār
honey: asal
honour: efte<u>kh</u>ār, <u>sh</u>araf, āberu; **word of honour**, <u>gh</u>owle <u>sh</u>araf
hook: <u>gh</u>ollab; gire
hope *n*: omid
horizon: ofo<u>gh</u>
horn: bu<u>gh</u>
horse: asb
hospital: bimārestan, mariz<u>kh</u>āne
hot: dā<u>gh</u>

hotel: mehmānkhāne, hotel
hour: sā'at
house: khāne
how: chetowr
human: ensāni
hunger: gorosnegi
hurry *n*: ajale
hurt: *vb* (*intrans.*) dard āmadan (ā), dard kardan (kon); (*trans.*)
 dard āvardan (ār)
husband: showhar
hut: kolbe
hyacinth: sonbol
hygiene: behdāsht

I: man
ice: yakh
ice-cream: bastani
idea: nazar, fekr, ide
if: agar
ignorance: nādāni, jahālat
ignorant: jāhel, nādān
ill: mariz, nākhosh, bimār
illegal: ghêire ghānuni
illiterate: bi savād
illness: nākhoshi, bimāri
immediate: fowri
immune: masun
impartial: bitaraf
impatient: bihowsele, ajul
import *vb*: vāred kardan (kon)
important: mohem
impossible: ghêire momken
imprison: habs kardan (kon)
improve: (*intrans.*) behtar shodan (shav); (*trans.*) behtar kardan
 (kon)
in: dar, tu(ye)
income: darāmad
increase: (*intrans.*) ziād shodan (shav); (*trans.*) ziād kardan (kon)
independence: esteghlāl

independent: mostaghel
India: hendustān
Indian: hendi
indicate: eshāre kardan (kon)
industry: san'at (*pl.* sanāye')
inexperienced: bi tajrobe
infectious: mosri
infidel: kāfar
inflation: tavarrom
influenza: ānfluānzā
inform: ettelā' dādan (deh)
information: ettelā' (*pl.* ettelā'at), khabar (*pl.* akhbār)
injection: āmpul
injure: zakhmi kardan (kon)
ink: jowhar
innocent: bi gonāh
insects: hasharāt
inside: dākhel(e)
insist: esrār kardan (kon)
inspector: bāzras
install: kār gozāshtan (gozār)
instalment: ghest
instead of: bejāye
insurance: bime
intelligent: bā hush, āghel
interesting: jāleb
international: beînolmelali
interpreter: motarjem
interval: fāsele; (*pause*) tanaffos
interview *n*: mosāhebe
intestine: rude
into: dar
introduce: mo'arrefi kardan (kon)
invent: ekhterā' kardan (kon)
invitation: da'vat
invite: da'vat kardan (kon)
iron: (*metal*) āhan; (*for ironing*) utu
irrigate: āb dādan (deh)
Islam: eslām

Islamic: eslāmi
island: jazire
Italian: itālyā'i
Italy: itālya
itch: *n* khāresh; *vb* khāridan (khār)

jacket: kot, zhāket
jam: morabbā
jasmine: yās
jaw: ārvāre
Jesus: hazrate isā
Jew: kalimi, yāhudi, juhud
jewel: javāher
Jewish: kalimi, yāhudi, juhud
joint: (*anatomical*) mafsal
joke *n*: shukhi
jolt: takān
jumper: pulover
journalist: ruznāme negar
journey: safar, mosāferat
judge: *n* ghāzi, dādras; *vb* ghezāvat kardan (kon)
juice: āb
jump *vb*: paridan (par)
jury: hey'ate monsefe
just: (*equitable*) ādel
justice: edālat

keep: negah dāshtan (dār)
keepsake: yādegāri
kernel: haste
kerosene: naft
kettle: ketri
key: kilid
kick *vb*: lagad kardan (kon), lagad zadan (zan)
kidney: kolye; (*edible*) gholve
kill: koshtan (kosh)
kind: *adj* mehrabān; *n* now', jens
kindergarten: kudakestān
king: shāh, pādeshāh

kiss *n*: buse, mā<u>ch</u>
kitchen: ā<u>sh</u>paz<u>kh</u>āne
kitten: ba<u>chch</u>e gorbe
knee: zānu
kneel: zānu zadan (zan)
knife: <u>ch</u>ā<u>gh</u>u, kard
knit: bāftan (bāf)
knock *vb*: dar zadan (zan)
knot *n*: gere
know: dānestan (dān)
Koran: <u>gh</u>or'ān

label: bar <u>ch</u>asb, etiket
laboratory: āzmāye<u>sh</u>gāh
ladder: nardebān
lady: <u>kh</u>ānum, bānu
lake: daryā<u>ch</u>e
lamb: barre
lame: <u>sh</u>al, <u>ch</u>olā<u>gh</u>
lamp: <u>ch</u>erā<u>gh</u>
landlord/lady: sāheb<u>kh</u>āne (*coll.* sāb<u>kh</u>une)
language: zabān
lantern: fānus, <u>ch</u>erā<u>gh</u>
last: *adj* ā<u>kh</u>ar, ā<u>kh</u>arin; **last week**, hafteye gozashte; **at last**,
    bel'a<u>kh</u>are; *vb* (*be durable*) bā davām budan (bā<u>sh</u>), davām
    dā<u>sh</u>tan (dār)
late: dir
laugh *n*: <u>kh</u>ande
lavatory: mostarā, tuālet
law: <u>gh</u>ānun
lawyer: vakil
lazy: tambal
lead *vb*: rahbari kardan (kon); (*show the way*) rāhnamā'i kardan
    (kon)
leader: rahbar
leaf: barg
leak *vb*: āb dādan (deh)
lean *vb*: takye dādan
leap year: sāle kabise

learn: yād gereftan (gir), āmukhtan (āmuz)
least: kamtarin; **at least**, aghallan
leather: charm
leave *vb*: tark kardan (kon), raftan (rav); **to leave behind**, jā
  gozāshtan (gozār)
leek: tare farangi
left: chap
leg: pā
lemon: limu
lend: gharz dādan (deh), vām dādan
length: tul
lentil: adas
leopard: palang
less: kamtar
lesson: dars
letter: nāme; (*of the alphabet*) harf (*pl.* horuf)
lettuce: kāhu
liar: dorughgu
library: ketābkhāne
licence: javāz, tasdigh, ejāze
lick: lisidan (lis)
lid: sarpush, dar
lie *n*: dorugh
life: zendegi
lift: *vb* boland kardan; *n* (*elevator*) asānsor
light: *n* nur; rowshanā'i; cherāgh; *adj* (*not dark*) rowshan; (*in
  weight*) sabok
lightning: bargh
like: mesle, mānande; (*resembling*) shabih; *vb* (*people, things*)
  dust dāshtan (dār); (*want to do*) meîl dāshtan (dār)
lilac: yās
limit *n*: hadd
limited: mahdud
line: khat
lining: āstar
lion: shir
lip: lab
listen: gush kardan (kon); gush dādan (deh)
little: kuchak (*coll.* kuchik)

live *vb*: zendegi kardan (kon)
live *adj*: zende
liver: kabed; (*edible*) jegar
load *n*: bār
loan *n*: gharz, vām
local: mahalli
lock *n*: ghofl
locksmith: ghoflsāz
locust: malakh
loin cloth: long
long: derāz, tavil, tulāni; **how long?**, chand vaght?; **long ago**, khêîli vaght pish; **to take a long time**, tul keshidan (kesh)
look: *n* negāh; *vb* negāh kardan (kon)
loose: shol
lorry: kāmyon
lose: gom kardan (kon); (*a game*) bākhtan (bāz)
loss: ziān, zarar
losses: (*casualties*) talafāt
loud: boland
loudspeaker: bolandgu
love: *n* eshgh; *vb* dust dāshtan (dār); **to be in love**, āshegh budan (bāsh)
low: past; (*quiet*) yavāsh
lower: pā'in āvardan (ār)
luck: shāns
luggage: bār, asbāb
lukewarm: velarm
lunar: ghamari
lunch: nāhār
lung: rie

machine gun: mosalsal
machinery: māshinālat
mad: divāne (*coll.* divune)
magazine: majalle
magnet: āhanrobā
main: asli
maize: zorrat
major: (*mil.*) sargord

majority: aksariyat
make: dorost kardan (kon), sākhtan (sāz)
man: mard; (*mankind*) ādam, ādamizād
manager: modir
manual: (*by hand*) dasti
manufacture *vb*: sākhtan (sāz)
many: khêili, ziād
map: naghshe
marble: marmar
march: (*in a demonstration*) rāhpêimā'i
mark *n*: alāmat
market: bāzār
marriage: ezdevāj, arusi
marrow: (*vegetable*) kadu
marry: ezdevāj kardan (kon), arusi kardan
martyr: shahid
matches: kebrit
material: pārche
mathematics: riāziyāt
mattress: doshak
mauve: banafsh
mayor: shahrdār
measure: andāze; *vb* andāze gereftan (gir)
meat: gusht
meddle: fuzuli kardan (kon), dekhālat kardan (kon)
medical: pezeshki, tebbi
medicine: davā, dāru
meet: molāghāt kardan (kon); (*welcome*) esteghbāl kardan (kon)
meeting: molāghāt; (*of committee etc.*) jalese
melon: garmak, tālebi, kharboze
melt: āb shodan (shav)
memory: hāfeze
merchant: tājer, bāzargān
mercy: rahm
message: pêighām, peyām
metal: felez
midday: zohr
middle: vasat
Middle East: khāvare miāne

midnight: nesfeshab, nimeshab
mild: molāyem
military: nezāmi
milk: shir
million: melyun
mind: aghl
mine *n*: ma'dan; (*explosive*) min
mineral *adj*: ma'dani
minister: (*govt*) vazir
ministry: vezārat
minority: aghalliyat
minus: menhā
minute: daghighe
miracle: mo'jeze
mirror: āyne
miss: *n* (*unmarried woman*) dushize; *vb* (*bus etc.*) az dast dādan;
    I miss you, delam barāt tang shode
mix *vb*: ghāti kardan (kon), makhlut kardan
model *n*: nemune, model
modern: jadid, modern, motejadded
moisture: rotubat
Monday: doshambe
money: pul
monkey: meîmun
month: māh
moon: māh
moonlight: mahtāb
more: bishtar
morning: sob
mosque: masjed
mosquito: pashe
moth: bid, shāpare
mother: mādar
mother-in-law: (*wife's mother*) mādar zan; (*husband's mother*)
    mādar showhar
motor-bike: motorsiklet
mountain: kuh
mourn: azā gereftan (gir); azādāri kardan (kon)
mouse: mush

moustache: sibil
mouth: dahān (*coll*. dahan)
move *vb*: harekat kardan; **to move house**, asbābkeshi kardan (kon)
movement: harekat
much: khêıli, ziād
mud: gel
mulberry: tut
mule: ghāter
mullah: ākhund
muscle: azole
museum: muze
mushroom: ghārch
music: musighi
Muslim: mosalmān
must: bāyad
mustard: khardal
mutton: gushte gusfand

nail: mikh; **fingernail**, nākhun
name: esm, nām
nap: chort
napkin: dastmāl sofre
narcissus: narges
narrow: bārik, tang
nation: mellat
national: melli
nationality: melliyyat
natural: tabi'i
naughty: shêıtān
navy: niruye daryā'i
near: nazdik
nearly: taghriban
necessary: lāzem
neck: gardan
necklace: gardanband
nectarine: shalil
need: *n* ehtiāj; *vb* lāzem dāshtan (dār)
needle: suzan
negotiate: mo'āmele kardan (kon)

negro: siāhpust
neighbour: hamsāye
neither . . . nor: na . . . na
nephew: (*brother's child*) barādar zāde; (*sister's child*) khāhar zāde
nerve: asab (*pl.* a'sāb)
net: tur
never: hargez, hichvaght
new: now, jadid, tāze
news: khabar (*pl.* akhbār)
newspaper: ruznāme
New Year: sāle now, now ruz
next: ba'di
niece: (*sister's child*) khāhar zāde; (*brother's child*) barādar zāde
night: shab
nightingale: bolbol
nine: noh
nineteen: nuzdah
ninety: navad
no: na, khêir
noise: sedā
nonsense: mozakhraf, charand
noon: zohr
no one: hichkas
normal: āddi, ma'muli, normāl
north: shomāl
nose: damāgh, bini
notary: mahzardār, daftardār; (*lawyer*) vakil
note *n*: yaddāsht
note-book: daftarche, daftare yāddāsht
nothing: hich, hichchi (+ *negative verb*)
notice *vb*: tavajjoh kardan (kon), motevajjeh shodan (shav)
notify: ettelā' dādan (deh), khabar dādan
nought: sefr, hich
noun: esm
now: hālā
nuisance: mozāhem; asbābe zahmat
numb: bihess, serr
number: shomāre, adad
nurse *n*: parastār

oak: balut
oath: ghasam, sowgand
obedience: etā'at
object *n*: (*thing*) shey'; (*aim*) hadaf
object *vb*: e'terāz kardan (kon)
occupied: eshghāl; mashghul
ocean: oghyānus
oculist: cheshm pezeshk
odd: (*number*) tāgh; (*strange*) ajib
of: az
off: az; **far off**, dur
offend: ranjāndan (ranjān); **to be offended**, ranjidan (ranj)
offer: *n* (*proposal*) pishnahād; *vb* pishnahād kardan; (*a gift*) hedye kardan
office: edāre, daftar; (*position*) post, maghām
officer: afsar
official: *adj* rasmi; *n* ma'mur
often: bārhā, ziād
oil: rowghan; (*petroleum*) naft
old: (*of people*) pir; (*of things*) kohne
olive: zêitun; **olive oil**, rowghan zêitun
on: ruye
once: yek bār, yek daf'e
one: yek
onion: piāz
only: faghat
open *adj*: bāz
operation: (*medical*) amal (e jarrahi); (*military*) amaliyyāt
opinion: aghide
opium: taryāk
opportunity: forsat
opposite: (*facing*) ruberu(ye), moghābel(e)
or: yā; **either . . . or** yā . . . yā
oral: shafāhi
orange: portaghāl
order: *n* (*arrangement*) tartib; (*command*) amr, farmān; **out of order**, kharāb; *vb* (*goods, food*) sefāresh dādan (deh)
ordinary: ma'muli
organisation: sāzemān

original: asl, asli
orphan: yatim
other: digar (*coll.* dige)
otherwise: dar ghêire insurat
ought: bāyad (+ *subjunctive*)
out: birun, khārej
outside: birun, birune
oven: fer; tanur (*hole in ground or wall*)
over: bālāye, ruye
overalls: rupush
overcoat: pālto
overflow *vb*: sav raftan
overtake: jelow zadan (zan)
owl: joghd
own *vb*: dāshtan (dār)
owner: sāheb
ox: gāv

pack *vb*: bastan (band); baste bandi kardan (kon)
package: baste
page: safhe
pain: dard
painter: naghghāsh
painting: naghghāshi
pair: (*two of something*) joft
palace: ghasr, kākh
pale: (*colours*) rowshan, kamrang; (*face*) rang paride
palm: (*of hand*) kafe dast; (*tree*) nakhl
pansy: banafshe
pants: zir shalvāri
paper: kāghaz
paradise: behesht
parcel: baste
parents: pedar o mādar; vāledêin
park: *n* pārk; **car park**, pārking; *vb* pārk kardan (kon)
parsley: ja'fari
part: ghesmat
partridge: kabk
partner: sharik

party: (*social gathering*) mehmuni; (*political*) hezb
pass *vb*: (*an exam*) g͟habul s͟hodan; (*to pass by*) rad s͟hodan az;
   note that rad s͟hodan *by itself means to fail* (*an exam, test etc.*)
passenger: mosāfer
passport: gozarnāme, pāsport
past: goza͟shte
patience: sabr, howsele
patient: *adj* sabur; *n* (*sick person*) mariz
pavement: piāderow
pay *vb*: pul dādan (deh)
pea: (*chick pea*) nok͟hod; (*green pea*) nok͟hod farangi
peace: solh
peach: hulu
peacock: tāvus
pear: golābi
pearl: morvārid
peel: *n* pust; *vb* pust kandan (kan)
pen: g͟halam
pencil: medād
people: mardom
pepper: felfel
percent: darsad
perfect: bi êib, kāmel
perfume: atr
perhaps: s͟hāyad (+ *subjunctive*)
permit: *n* javāz; *vb* ejāze dādan (deh)
Persia: irān
Persian: (*the people and things*) irāni; (*the language*) fārsi
person: s͟hak͟hs
perspire: arag͟h kardan (kon)
petrol: benzin
petrol station: pompe benzin
petroleum: naft
pharmacy: dārukhāne, davākhāne
photograph: aks
photography: akkāsi
pickles: tors͟hi
picture: aks
piece: tekke, g͟hat'e

pierce: surākh kardan (kon)
pig: khuk
pigeon: kabutar
pilgrim: zavvār; (*to Mecca*) hāji
pilgrimage: ziārat; (*to Mecca*) hājj
pilot: (*of aeroplane*) khalabān
pill: ghors
pillow: bālesh
pin: sanjāgh
pink: surati
pipe: pip, chopogh
pity: *n* tarahom; **it's a pity** hêif-e; *vb* delsuzi kardan
place *n*: jā
plain *adj*: sāde; (*clear*) vāzeh
plan *n*: naghshe
plant *n*: giyāh
plaster: gach
plate: boshghāb
play *vb*: bāzi kardan (kon)
please *vb*: rāzi kardan (kon)
plenty: farāvān
plum: ālu
plumber: lulekesh
plural: jam'
pocket: jib
poem: she'r
poet: shā'er
point: *n* sar, nok; (*dot*) noghte; (*nicety*) nokte; *vb* neshān dādan, eshāre kardan
pole: ghotb
police: polis; **police officer**, afsare polis
policeman: pasebān
police station: kalāntari
polite: bā adab, bā tarbiat
political: siāsi
politics: siāsat
pomegranate: anār
pond: howz
poor: faghir

Pope: pāp
population: jam'iyyat
port: bandar
porter: (*for luggage*) bārbar; (*door-keeper*) darbān
possess: dāshtan (dār)
possible: momken
post *n*: post
postage stamp: tambr
post office: postkhāne
pot: (*saucepan*) dig; (*flower pot*) goldān
potato: sibe zamini (*coll.* sibzamini)
pour: rikhtan (riz)
power: ghodrat, niru
practise: tamrin kardan (kon)
pray: do'ā kardan (kon)
prayer: do'ā
prefer: tarjih dādan (deh)
pregnant: ābestan, hāmele
prepare: āmāde kardan (kon)
prescription: noskhe
present: *adj* hāzer; (*now*) hālā; *n* (*gift*) kādo, hedye
press: *n* the press: matbu'āt; *vb* feshār dādan (deh)
pressure: feshār
pretty: khoshgel
price: bahā, ghêimat
pride: ghorur, takabbor; (*in the good sense*) eftekhār
priest: keshish
prime minister: nakhost vazir
print *vb*: chāp kardan (kon)
priority: taghaddom
prison: zendān, habs
private: khosusi
probable: momken
problem: mas'ale
produce: *n* mahsul; *vb* towlid kardan (kon)
production: towlid
professor: ostād
profit: sud, naf', manfa'at
programme: barnāme

progress *n*: pishraft, taraggi
promise *n*: ghowl, va'de
pronunciation: talaffoz
prophet: pêighambar, rasul
proposal: pishnahād
protect: hemāyat kardan (kon)
protest *vb*: e'terāz kardan (kon)
proud: maghrur
prove: sābet kardan (kon)
public: omumi
pull: keshidan (kesh)
pulse: nabz
pump: tolombe
puncture: panchar
punish: tanbih kardan (kon)
puppy: tule sag
pure: khāles
purple: banafsh
purse: kife pul
push: hol dādan (deh)
put: gozāshtan (gozar)

quality: jens
quantity: meghdār
quarrel: da'vā
quarter: (*numerical*) rob'; (*part of a town*) mahalle
queen: maleke
question *n*: so'āl
quick: (*fast*) tond; (*soon*) zud
quiet *adj*: sāket, arām
quilt: lāhāf

rabbit: khargush
race *n*: (*competition*) mosābeghe; (*nationality*) nezhād
radio: rādio
radish: torobche
railway: rāhe āhan, rāhāhan; **railway station**, istgāhe rāhāhan
rain *n*: bārān
rainbow: ghowsoghazah

raincoat: bārāni
raisin: keshmesh
raw: khām
razor: tigh
reach: residan (res)
read: khāndan (khān)
ready: hāzer
real: vāghe'i
reason *n*: dalil, ellat
receipt: resid
recognise: shenākhtan (shenās)
recommendation: towsiye
record *vb*: zabt kardan (kon)
recreation: tafrih
red: ghermez, sorkh
reduce: kam kardan (kon)
refine: tasfiye kardan
refinery: palāyeshgāh
refuge: panāh, panāhgāh
refugee: panāhande
refuse *vb*: ghabul nakardan (nakon), rad kardan (kon)
regret *n*: ta'assof
regular: morattab
relations: (*kindred*) ghomokhish, fāmil; (*proportion*) nesbat;
    diplomatic relations, ravābete siāsi
religion: mazhab, din
remember: yād dāshtan (dār); **I remember**, yādam miāyad/miād
remind: yādāvari kardan (kon)
repeat *vb*: tekrār kardan (kon)
repent: towbe kardan (kon)
reply *vb*: javāb dādan (deh)
report *n*: gozāresh
representative: namāyande
republic: jomhuri
request *n*: darkhāst, taghāzā
rescue *n*: nejāt
resemblance: shabāhat
reserve *vb*: jā gereftan (gir), rezerv kardan (kon)
resign: este'fā dādan (deh) *or* kardan (kon)

respect *n*: ehterām
responsible: mas'ul
result *n*: natije
retire: bāzneshaste <u>sh</u>odan (<u>sh</u>av)
return *vb*: bā<u>z</u> ga<u>sh</u>tan (gard), bar ga<u>sh</u>tan (gard)
revenge: ente<u>gh</u>ām
revolution: en<u>gh</u>elāb
reward *n*: pādā<u>sh</u>
rhubarb: rivās
rib: dande
ribbon: rubān
rice: berenj
rich: puldār, motemavvel
ride *vb*: savāri kardan (kon)
ridicule: *n* mas<u>kh</u>are; *vb* mas<u>kh</u>are kardan (kon)
riding: savāri
right: rāst, dorost, sahih
ring: *n* hal<u>gh</u>e; (*for the finger*) ango<u>sh</u>tar; *vb* (*bell*) zang zadan (zan)
rinse *vb* āb ke<u>sh</u>idan (ke<u>sh</u>)
ripe: reside
rise: boland <u>sh</u>odan (<u>sh</u>av)
river: rud<u>kh</u>āne
road: <u>kh</u>iābān, jādde, rāh
rob: dozdidan (dozd), dozdi kardan (kon)
roof: sa<u>gh</u>f, po<u>sh</u>te bām (*coll.* po<u>sh</u>tebun)
room: otā<u>gh</u>; (*space*) jā
root: ri<u>sh</u>e
rope: tanāb, rismān
rose: gole sor<u>kh</u>, roz
rot *vb*: pusidan (pus)
rough: zebr
round: gerd
rub: mālidan (māl)
rubber: lāstik; (*eraser*) medād pāk kon
rubbish: ā<u>sh</u>g<u>h</u>āl
rude: bi adab, bi tarbiat
rug: <u>gh</u>āliche
ruin *n*: <u>kh</u>arābi; (*a place*) virāne, <u>kh</u>arābe

rule *n*: ghā'ede
run *vb*: davidan (dav) (*coll.* dowidan)
rural: rustā'i
Russia: rusiye
Russian: rusi
rust: zang
rusty: zang zade

sack: guni
sacrifice: ghorbāni
sad: ghamgin
saddle: zin
safe: amn
safety: amniyyat
saffron: za'ferun
sail *n*: bādbān
sailor: malavān
salary: hoghugh (*pl. of* hagh = *right(s)*)
sale: forush; (*auction*) harāj
salmon: māhiye āzād
salt: namak
salt-cellar: namakdān
same: hamin, hamun
sample: nemune
sand: shen, māsse
Satan: shêitān
satellite: māhvāre
satisfaction: rezāyat
satisfy: rāzi kardan (kon)
Saturday: shambe
saucepan: ghābleme
saucer: nalbeki
savings: pasandāz
saw *n*: arre
say: goftan (gu)
scales: tarāzu
scarcely: benodrat
scarf: shalgardan; **headscarf**, rusari
school: madrese

science: elm (*pl.* olum)
scissors: ghêichi
scorpion: aghrab
scratch *vb*: khārāndan (khārān)
screw: pich
screwdriver: pichgushti, pichvākon
scythe: dās
sea: daryā; **seaside**, kenāre daryā
seal *n*: mohr
season: fasl
seat: sandali; (*in a cinema, theatre, etc.*) jā
second: *n* (*time*) sāniye; *adj* (*number*) dovvom
second-hand: daste dovvom
secret: *n* rāz; *adj* serri
secretary: monshi
security: amniyyat
see: didan (bin)
seed: tokhm, bazr
seldom: benodrat
sell: forukhtan (forush)
send: ferestādan (ferest)
sensible: āghel
sentence: jomle
separate: jodā, savā
servant: mostakhdem, kārgar
service: khedmat
seven: haft
seventeen: hivdāh
seventy: haftād
several: chand
sew: dukhtan (duz)
sewing: khayyāti
sewing machine: charkhe khayyāti
sex: jens
shade, shadow: sāye
shake: takān dādan (deh)
shallow: kam omgh
shame: sharm
shape: shekl, tarkib

share *n*: sahm (*pl.* sahām); **shared**, shariki, sherākati
shareholder: sahāmdār
sharp: tiz
sharpener: (*pencil sharpener*) medād tarāsh
shave: tarāshidan (tarāsh); (*one's beard*) rish tarāshidan (tarāsh)
sheep: gusfand
sheet: (*for a bed*) malāfe; (*of paper*) varagh
shelf: tāghche
shepherd: chupān
ship: kashti
shirt: pirhan
shiver: larzidan (larz)
shoe: kafsh
shoehorn: pāshnekesh
shoelace: bande kafsh
shoemaker: kaffāsh
shoot: bā tir zadan (zan); tirandāzi kardan (kon)
shop: *n* maghāze, dokkān; *vb* kharid kardan (kon)
shopkeeper: maghāzedār, dokkāndār
short: kutā
short-sighted: nazdikbin
shoulder: shāne
show *vb*: neshān dādan (deh)
shut *vb*: bastan (band)
shy: khejālati
sick: mariz, bimār
side: pahlu, taraf, kenār
sieve: *n* sāfi, alak; *vb* sāf kardan, alak kardan (kon)
sign, signal *n*: alāmat
signature: emzā
silence: sokut
silk: abrisham
silver: noghre
similarity: shabāhat
simple: sāde
sin *n*: gonāh
since: (*because*) chun; (*time*) az vaghtike
sing: āvāz khāndan (khān)
single: tak

sister: khāhar
sister-in-law: (*wife's sister*) khāhar zan; (*husband's sister*) khāhar showhar
sit: neshastan (neshin)
sitting room: otāghe neshiman
six: shesh
sixteen: shunzdah
sixty: shast
size: andāze
skin: pust
skirt: dāman
sky: āsemān
slap *n*: keshide
sleep *vb*: khābidan (khāb)
sleet: burān
sleeve: āstin
slide *vb*: sor khordan, liz khordan (khor)
slipper: dampā'i
slow: āheste, yavāsh
small: kuchak
smallpox: ābele
smell *n*: bu
smile *n*: labkhand
smoke: *n* dud; *vb* (*fire etc*) dud kardan (kon); (*cigarettes*) sigār keshidan (kesh)
smooth: sāf
snake: mār
sneeze: *n* atse; *vb* atse kardan (kon)
snore *vb*: khor khor kardan (kon)
snow *n*: barf
so: banābar'in
soap: sābun
society: jāme'e, ejtemā'
sock: jurāb
sofa: nimkat, mobl
soft: narm
soil: khāk
solar: khorshidi, shamsi
soldier: sarbāz

some: ba'zi
somebody: yek kas, kasi
something: yek chiz, chizi
sometimes: gāhi, ba'zi vaghthā
somewhere: jā'i, yek jā
son: pesar
song: āvāz, tarāne
son-in-law: dāmād
soon: zud, bezudi
sorry: mota'assef; **I am sorry**, bebakhshid
soup: sup
sour: torsh
south: jonub
souvenir: yādegāri
Soviet Union: showravi; **USSR**, ettehāde jamāhire showravi
sow: kāshtan (kār)
space: (*room*) jā, fazā; (*outer space*) fazā
spade: bil
Spain: espānyā
Spanish: espānyoli
spanner: āchār
spare *adj*: ezāfi, yadak; **spare wheel**, charkhe yadak
speak: harf zadan (zan); sohbat kardan (kon)
special: makhsus
spectacles: êinak
speech: sohbat; (*at a rally etc.*) sokhanrāni
speed *n*: sor'at
spend: (*money*) kharj kardan (kon); (*time*) gozarāndan (gozar); sarf kardan (kon)
spice *n*: adviyye
spill: rikhtan (riz)
spinach: esfenāj
spoil: (*trans.*) kharāb kardan (kon); (*intrans.*) kharāb shodan (shav)
spoon: ghāshogh
sport: varzesh
spring: (*season*) bahār
square: *n* mêidān; *adj* chahārgush
stair: pelle

stamp: (*postage*) tambr; (*seal*) mohr
stand: istādan (ist)
star: setāre
station: railway station, istgāhe rāhāhan
statue: mojassame
stay: māndan (mān)
steal: dozdidan (dozd)
steam: bokhār
step: ghadam; (*of a stair*) pelle
step-brother: nā barādari
step-daughter: nā dokhtari
step-father: nā pedari
step-mother: nā mādari
step-son: nā pesari
stick: (*intrans.*) chasbidan (chasb); (*trans.*) chasbāndan
sticky: nuch, chasbnāk
still: *adj* ārām; *adv* (*yet*) hanuz
sting *n*: nish
stir: ham zadan (zan)
stocking: jurāb
stomach: shekam, ma'de
stone: sang
stop *vb*: (*intrans.*) istādan (ist); negah dāshtan (dār); **to stop doing sth.**, nakardan
storey: tabaghe; **multi-storey**, chand tabaghe
storm: tufān
story: dāstān, ghesse
straight: rāst, sāf
strawberry: tutfarangi
stream: nahr, juy
street: kuche
string: nakh
student: dāneshju; mohassel
study *vb*: dars khāndan (khān)
stupid: ahmagh
sturgeon: māhiye uzun borun; māhiye khāviar
subtract: kam kardan (kon)
suburb: hume
such: chenin

suck: mekidan (mek)
sudden: nāgahāni, (*coll.*) yeho
sugar: shekar; (*lump sugar*) ghand
suicide: khodkoshi
suit: (*man's*) kotshalvār; (*woman's*) kotdāman
sum: (*of money*) mablagh
summer: tābestān
sun: āftāb
Sunday: yekshambe
sunrise: tolu'e āftāb
sunset: ghorube āftāb
supermarket: supermārket
supper: shām
suppose: tasavvor kardan (kon); gamān kardan (kon)
sure: motma'en
surgeon: jarrāh
surprise: ta'ajjob
swallow *vb*: ghurt dādan (deh); bal'idan (bal')
sweat *n*: aragh
sweep: jāru kardan (kon)
sweet: shirin
swim: sheno kardan (kon)
swimming pool: estakhr
syringe: sorang
syrup: shire

table: miz; **table-cloth**, rumizi
tailor: khayyāt
take: gereftan (gir); **to take away**, bordan (bar); **to take off**
   (*clothes*) kandan (kan), dar āvardan (ār)
talk *vb*: harf zadan (zan); sohbat kardan (kon)
tall: boland
tangerine: nārengi
tap: shir
tape: navār
tape recorder: zabte sowt
tax *n*: māliāt
taxi: tāksi
tea: chā'i

teach: dars dādan (deh)
teacher: mo'allem, āmuzegār
tea-cup: fenjān
tear *vb*: pāre kardan (kon)
tears: ashk
tease: sar besar gozāshtan (gozār)
telegramme: telgerāf
telephone: telefon
television: televizyon
tell: goftan (gu)
temporary: movaghghat
ten: dah
tenant: mosta'jer
test *n*: āzmāyesh
than: az
thank: tashakkor kardan (kon)
that: ān
theft: dozdi
then: ānvaght
there: ānjā
therefore: banābar'in
these: inhā
they: ānhā
thick: koloft, zakhim
thief: dozd
thin: lāghar
thing: chiz (*pl.* chizhā), shêi' (*pl.* ashyā')
think: fekr kardan (kon)
third: sevvom
thirst: teshnegi
thirsty: teshne
this: in
those: ānhā
thought: fekr
thousand: hezār
three: se
throat: galu
through: az
throw *vb*: andākhtan (andāz); part kardan (kon)

thunder: ra'd
Thursday: panjshambe
thus: intowr
ticket: bilit
tie: *n* (*necktie*) kerāvāt; *vb* bastan (band); **to tie a knot**, gere zadan (zan)
tight: tang
tile: kāshi
till: (*until*) tā
time: vaght, zamān; **by the time that**, tā; **from time to time**, gāhi; (*the hour*) sā'at
tin: ghuti
tired: khaste
to: be
today: emruz
toe: angoshte pā
together: bā ham
tomato: gowje farangi
tomorrow: fardā
tongue: zabān
tonight: emshab
too: (*also*) ham; (*too much*) ziādi
tool: abzār
tooth: dandān
toothbrush: mesvāk
toothpaste: khamir dandān
torch: cherāgh ghovve
touch *vb*: dast zadan (zan)
tourist: jahāngard, turist
towards: be tarafe
towel: howle
town: shahr
trade: tejārat; (*craft or occupation*) herfe
traffic: raft o āmad, āmad o shod, terāfik
train *n*: teran, ghatār
transaction: mo'āmele
transfer *n*: enteghāl; (*of money*) havāle
translate: tarjome kardan (kon)
translation *n*: tarjome

transport *n*: haml o naghl; tarābari
travel: *n* mosāferat; *vb* mosāferat kardan (kon)
traveller: mosāfer
tree: derakht
tremble: larzidan (larz)
tribe: ghabile, il
trouble *n*: zahmat; **to take trouble**, zahmat keshidan (kesh);
  (*problems*) gereftāri, darde sar
trousers: shalvār
true: rāst
trunk: (*box*) sandogh; (*of a tree*) tane
trust *n*: e'temād, etminān
truth: rāsti, haghighat
Tuesday: seshambe
tulip: lāle
tune: āhang
turban: ammāme
Turk: tork
Turkey: Torkiyye
turkey: bughalamun
turmeric: zardchube
turn: *n* nowbat; *vb* pichāndan (pich); charkhāndan (charkh)
turnip: shalgham
turquoise: firuze; (*the colour*) firuzei
twelve: davāzdah
twenty: bist
twice: do daf'e, do bār
two: do
typewriter: māshine tahrir
typewriting: māshin nevisi
typhoid: hasbe
typist: māshin nevis

ugly: zesht
umbrella: chatr
unbeliever: kāfar
uncle: (*paternal*) amu; (*maternal*) dā'i
under: zire
under-secretary: mo'āven

understand: fahmidan (fahm)
unemployed: bikār
unemployment: bikāri
unfortunately: mota'asefāne
union: ettehād; (*of workers*) ettehādiye
unit: vāhed
United States: ayālāte mottahedeye āmrikā; āmrikā
university: dāneshgāh
unjust: bi ensāf
unless: magar, magar inke
untie: bāz kardan (kon)
up: bālā
upon: ruye
upper: bālā
upside-down: vārune
urgent: fowri
use: *n* it isn't any use, fāyede nadārad; *vb* masraf kardan (kon); estefāde kardan (kon) az; be kār bordan (bar)
useful: mofid, bedard bekhor
USSR: ettehāde jamāhire showravi
utensils: zarfhā, zoruf (*Arabic pl.*)
utmost: nahāyat

vacany: jā, jāye khāli
vacant: (*empty*) khāli; (*free*) āzād
vaccinate: māye kubi kardan (kon), vāksin zadan (zan)
valid: mo'tabar
valley: darre
valuable: ghêimati, arzande
value *n*: arzesh
vase: goldān
various: mokhtalef
veal: gushte gusāle
vegetables: sabzijāt (*Arabic pl.*)
veil: (*for the face*) rubande; (*long black veil*) chādor
vein: rag
verb: fe'l
very: khêili
vest: pirhan zir

victory: fath
video: vidyo
view: manzare
village: deh, dehkade, ābādi, rustā
vine: mow
vinegar: serke
visa: vizā, ravādid
visit: *n* didan; *vb* didan kardan
voice: sedā
volcano: ātesh feshān
vomit *n*: estefrāgh
vote *vb*: rā'y dādan (deh)

wages: hoghugh (*pl. of* hagh)
waist: kamar
wait *vb*: sabr kardan (kon)
wake: (*trans.*) bidār kardan (kon); (*intrans.*) bidār shodan
walk *vb*: rāh raftan (rav)
walking: rāhpêımā'i
wall: divār
walnut: gerdu
want *vb*: khāstan (khāh)
war: jang
warm: garm
warmth: garmā
wash *vb*: shostan (shuy, *coll.* shur)
washing machine: māshine rakhtshu'i
waste *vb*: harām kardan (kon)
waterfall: ābshār
watering can: ābpāsh
water-melon: hendevāne
wave: *n* (*of the sea*) mowj; *vb* dast takān dādan (deh)
way: rāh, tarigh
we: mā
weak: za'if
weakness: za'f
wealth: dārā'i
weapon: aslahe
wear: pushidan (push)

weather: havā
Wednesday: chahārshambe
week: hafte
weep: gerye kardan (kon)
weigh: (*trans.*) keshidan (kesh), vazn kardan (kon); (*intrans.*)
  vazn dāshtan (dār)
weight: vazn, sangini
welcome *vb*: khoshāmad goftan (gu), khêıre maghdam goftan
well *adv*: khub
west: gharb
western: gharbi
wet: khis, tar
what: chi, che
whatever: harchi, harche
wheat: gandom
wheel: charkh
when: vaghtike; (*interrog.*) kêı
whenever: har vaght, har gāh
where: jā'ike; kojā
wherever: har kojā ke
which: ke
whichever: har kudum
while: dar hālike
whisper *vb*: zemzeme kardan (kon), zire lab goftan (gu), pech
  pech kardan (kon) (*coll.*)
whistle *n*: sut
white: sefid
who: ke; ki
whole: kāmel, tamām
why: cherā
wide: pahn, ariz
widow: bive
width: arz, pahnā
wife: zan, hamsar
wild: vahshi
willow: bid
win *vb*: bordan (bar), barande shodan (shav)
wind: bād
window: panjere

wine: sharāb
wing: bāl
wink *vb*: cheshmak zadan (zan)
winter: zemestān
wire: sim
wireless: rādio, bisim
wise: āghel
wish *n*: ārezu
with: bā
within: dākhel
without: bedune
witness: shāhed
woman: zan
wood: chub
wool: pashm; **woollen**, pashmi
word: kalame, loghat, vāzhe
work *n*: kār
worker: kārgar
workshop: kārgah
world: donyā
worth: arzesh
wound *n*: zakhm
wrap: pichidan (pich), pichāndan (pichān)
wrist: moch, moche dast
write: neveshtan (nevis)

yard: hayāt; yārd (*English measure*)
year: sāl
yellow: zard
yes: bale, āre (*coll.*)
yesterday: diruz
yet: hanuz
you: to, shomā
young: javān
youth: javāni

zero: sefr
Zoroaster: zartosht
Zoroastrian: zartoshti (*coll.* zardoshti)

Persian – English Glossary

In this glossary ā, <u>ch</u>, <u>gh</u>, <u>kh</u>, <u>sh</u> and <u>zh</u> are treated as separate letters, following a, c, g, k, s and z respectively.

abad: eternity; **tā abad**, for ever; **abadi**, eternal
abr: cloud
abru: eyebrow
adab: manners; **bā adab**, polite; **bi adab**, rude
adabiyyāt: literature
adviyye: spice
afkār (*pl. of* **fekr**): thoughts
afsar: officer
afsus: what a pity

agar: if
aghab: behind
aghallan: at least
aghlab: mostly, often
aghrab: scorpion
ahmagh: stupid
ahyānan: by any chance
ajnās (*pl. of* **jens**): goods
akhiran: recently, lately
akhlāgh: temperament; **bad akhlāgh**, bad tempered; <u>**khosh**</u> **akhlāgh**, good tempered
akhm: frown; **akhm kardan (kon)**, to frown
akkās: photographer
aks: picture, photograph
aksaran: mostly, mainly
aksariyyat: majority
alaf: grass (*usually* long grass); weeds
al'ān: right now
albatte: of course
allāh: God (*Arabic*)
almās: diamond
amal: action (*pl.* **a'māl**); surgical operation (*pl.* **amalhā**)
amaliyyāt: operations

amānat: something lent or entrusted to someone (*can be things or money*)

ambār: store room; **ambār kardan (kon)**, to store, to accumulate

ammā: but

amr: command; **amr kardan, amr farmudan**, to command (*someone to do something*)

amrāz (*pl. of* **maraz**): diseases

an'ām: tip, gratuity

anār: pomegranate

andākhtan (andāz): to throw

andāze: size

angosht: finger

angoshtar: ring (*for finger*)

angulak kardan (kon): to fiddle with, to poke, to bait

angur: grape

anjir: fig

aragh: sweat; any distilled spirits e.g. **araghe keshmesh**, an alcohol distilled from raisins

arbāb: master

armani: Armenian

arre: saw

artesh: army

arus: bride

arusi: wedding

arz: foreign exchange; **arzi dāshtam**, polite way of saying 'I would like to say something'

arzān: inexpensive

arzesh: value, worth

asā: walking stick

asab (*pl.* **a'sāb**): nerve; **a'sābam kharāb-e**, my nerves are bad

asar: effect (*pl.* **āsār** is also used in **āsāre tārikhi**, historical remains)

asās: basis

asāsi: basic

asāsiye: furniture

asb: horse

asbāb: goods, furniture; **asbāb asāsiye**, goods & chattels

asir (*pl.* **osarā**): prisoner

asl (*pl.* **osul**): principle; **asli**, principal

aslahe: weapon
aslan: not at all (*with negative verb*)
asr: early evening, late afternoon
assä'e: right now
atr: perfume
aträf (*pl. of* **taraf**): side; **aträfe Tehrän**, around Tehran
avaz kardan (kon): to change (*trans.*), to exchange
avaz <u>sh</u>odan (<u>shav</u>): to change (*intrans.*)
avval: first
avvalan: firstly
az: from
azän: the call to prayer
aziat kardan (kon): to bother, to trouble (*trans.*)
aziz: dear

āb: water
āb ke<u>sh</u>idan (ke<u>sh</u>): to rinse
ābād: cultivated
ābādi: village
ābān: Aban, the 8th Persian month
ābele: smallpox
āberu: reputation; **āberum raft**, I lost face, I was disgraced
āberurizi: a disgrace (*lit.* the spilling of face water!)
ābi: blue
ābke<u>sh</u>: colander
ābpa<u>ch</u>: watering can
ābpaz: boiled (*of food, lit.* watercooked)
ā<u>ch</u>ār: spanner
ādat: habit, custom
āftāb: sun
āftābe: a kind of ewer for water, used specifically for washing
  instead of lavatory paper
āgahi: advertisement
āhan: iron (*the metal*)
āhang: tune
āhangar: blacksmith
āheste: slow, quiet
ājor: brick
ā<u>kh</u>ar: last

ākhund: mullah

ālbālu: a kind of cherry (*small, dark and sour, used for jam and in a rice dish*)

āli: very good, superb

ālmān: Germany

ālu: plum

āmadan (ā): to come

āmāde: ready

āmār: statistics

āmpul: injection

āmrikā: America

āmukhtan (āmuz): to learn

āmuzesh: learning

ān: that

ānjā: there

ārām: quiet, still

ārd: flour

āre: yes (*coll.*)

ārezu: wish

āsān: easy; **āsāni**, ease; **be āsuni**, easily

āsemān: sky

āsfālt: asphalt

āsh: Persian soup – it is usually quite thick and there are innumerable varieties

āshnā: acquaintance; acquainted

āshpaz: cook

āsyā: Asia

ātesh (*coll.* **ātish**): fire

āteshfeshān: volcano

āteshneshāni: fire brigade

āvardan (ār): to bring

āvāz khāndan (khān): to sing

āvizan kardan (kon): to hang (*things, trans.*); **āvizān**, hanging

āyande: future

āyne: mirror

āzād: free

āzar: Azar, 9th Persian month; girl's name

āzār: hurt, damage

āzmāyesh: test, trial

āzmāyeshgah: laboratory
āzhir: siren

bachche: child
bad: bad
ba'd: then, afterwards; **ba'd az**, after
baghghāl: grocer
baghiyye: remainder; **baghiyye(ye)**, the rest of
bahā: price
bahār: spring
bahman: 11th Persian month; boy's name; avalanche
bakhshidan (bakhsh): to forgive
bakhshesh: forgiveness
bakht: luck, fortune
balad budan (bāsh): to know (*how to do sth., a language etc.*)
bale: yes
banafsh: violet
banfshe: pansy
bandar (*pl.* **banāder**): port
bande: slave; *polite form for* I, i.e. your slave
bannā: builder
barābar: equal
barādar: brother
barāye: for
bar dāshtan (dār): to take off, to take away
bar gashtan (gard): to return, to turn around
barg: leaf
bargh: electricity
barnāme: programme
bas: enough
basij: mobilisation
bastan (band): to close, to tie, to fasten
bastani: ice cream
baste: parcel; *adj* closed
ba'zi: some
bā: with; **bā ham**, together
bād: wind; swelling; **bād kardan**, to swell
bādām: almond
bāgh: garden

bāghlavā: sweetmeat made of thin pastry, ground almonds and sugar

bāje: ticket office

bākhtan (bāz): to lose (*a game etc.*)

bāl: wing

bālā: up, above

bālesh: pillow

bālkon: balcony

bānk: bank

bānu: lady

bār: load, luggage; bar; times

bārān (*coll.* **bārun**): rain

bārāni (*coll.* **bāruni**): raincoat

bārik: narrow

bāsavād: literate

bāvar kardan (kon): to believe

bāz: open; **bāz kardan (kon)**, to open

bāzār: market, bazaar

bāzargān: merchant

bāzdid: control, inspection, return visit

bāzi: game

bāzras: inspector

bāzu: forearm

be: to

bedune: without

behesht: heaven, paradise

behdāsht: hygiene; public health

beine: between

beinolmelali: international

beiragh: flag

benzin: petrol

berenj: rice; brass

besyār: much, many, very

bi: without

biābun: uncultivated land, wasteland

bidār: awake; **bidār shodan**, to wake up; **bidār kardan (kon)**, to waken

bid: willow tree; clothes moth

bikhod: unnecessarily

bil: spade
bimār: sick
bimāri: sickness, illness
bime: insurance
bini: nose
birun: outside; **birun kardan (kon)**, to dismiss, to expel
bishtar: more
bist: twenty
bive: widow
bokhār: steam
bokhāri: fire, stove
boland: high, tall; **boland shodan (shav)**, to rise, to get up; **boland kardan (kon)**, to lift, to raise; (*coll.*) to steal
bolbol: nightingale
bombast: cul-de-sac
bordan (bar): to take away, to take, to carry
boridan (bor): to cut
boshghāb: plate
botri: bottle
boz: goat
bozorg: big, large, great
bu: smell; **bu kardan (kon)**, to smell (*trans.*); **bu dadan (deh)**, to smell (*intrans.*)
budan (bāsh): to be, to exist
bugh: horn
bus, buse: kiss; **busidan (bus)**, to kiss

chakkosh: hammer
chakme: boot
chaman: lawn, grass
chand: how much; how many; how long; some; few
changāl: fork; claw
chap: left
charb: greasy
charbi: grease, fat
charkh: wheel
charkhidan (charkh): to turn
charm: leather
chasb: glue

chasbidan: to stick
chashm: alright, certainly (*in answer to a command*)
chatr: umbrella
chādor: tent; the long veil worn by the women in Iran
chāi: tea
chāgh: fat (*adj*)
chāghu: knife
chāh: well (*n*)
chahār (*coll.* **chār**): four
chāp: print
chehel: forty
chek: cheque
chenār: plane tree
cherā: why
cherāgh: lamp
cherk: dirt, pus; dirty; **cherk kardan (kon)**, to become infected
   (*of wounds, lesions etc.*)
cheshidan (chesh): to taste
cheshm: eye
cheshmak: wink; **cheshmak zadan (zan)**, to wink
cheshme: spring
chetowr: how
chi: what
chidan (chin): to cut
chin: fold; China
chini: Chinese; porcelain
chiz: thing
cholāgh: lame
chort: snooze
chub: wood
chubi: wooden
chune: chin; **chune zadan (zan)**, to bargain, to haggle
churuk: wrinkle; crumpled

dabestān: primary school
daf'e: time; **yek daf'e**, once; **daf'eye dige**, next time
daftar: exercise book; office
daghigh: accurate
daghighe (*coll.* **daighe**): minute

dah: ten

dahān (*coll.* **dahan**): mouth

damāgh: nose

dandān (*coll.* **dandun**): tooth

dande: rib; gear; cog

dar: door (*n*); in; **dar bāreye**, concerning, about

dareje: degree, rank

dard: pain; **dard kardan (kon)** (*intrans.*), to ache; **dard āvardan**
 (**ār**) (*trans.*), to hurt; **dard āmadan (ā)** (*intrans.*), to hurt;
 dardam āmad, it hurt me

dars: lesson

dast: hand; **dast dādan**, to shake hands; **dast bardāshtan (bardār)**,
 to stop, to desist; **daste kam**, at least; **az dast dādan**, to lose
 (*a loved one, a job etc; to lose things is* **gom kardan**)

daste: group, bunch

dastkesh: glove

dastmāl: handkerchief

davā: medicine

da'vā: argument; **da'vā kardan (kon)**, to argue, to quarrel

davāzdah: twelve

davidan (**dav**, *coll.* **dow**): to run

dādan (**deh**): to give

dādāsh: brother (*coll., also affectionate*)

dādgostari: justice; **vezārate dādgostari**, Ministry of Justice

dādsetān: public prosecutor; **dādsetāni**, the public prosecutor's
 office

dā'em, dā'emi: permanent, perpetual

dā'eman: perpetually, constantly

dāgh: hot

dāmād: son-in-law; bridegroom

dāman: skirt

dānestan (**dān**) (*coll.* **dun**): to know

dānesh: knowledge

dāneshāmuz: student (*usually in school*)

dāneshgah: university

dārchin: cinnamon

dāru: medicine

dāstān: story

dāshtan (**dār**): to have

dāyere: circle

deghghat: care; **deghghat kardan (kon)**, to pay attention, to take care

deh: village

del: heart, stomach

delsuzi: sympathy; **delam sukht**, I felt sorry; **delam barāsh sukht**, I felt sorry for him/it

deldard: stomach ache

delkhor: put out, offended

deltang: sad, distressed

derāz: long

dey: 10th Persian month

didan (bin): to see

didani: visiting

dig: cooking pot

digar (*coll.* **dige**): other, next; **daf'eye dige**, next time; **ruze dige**, another day; **chize dige**, something else

din: religion

dir: late; **dir kardan (kon)**, to be late

diruz: yesterday

dishab: last night

divāne (*coll.* **divune**): mad

divār: wall

dokhtar: girl; daughter

dokkān (*coll.* **dokkun**): shop

dokkāndār: shopkeeper

dogme: button

donyā: world

dorost: correct, right; **dorost kardan (kon)**, to make, to put right

doroste: whole

dorugh: lie, falsehood; **dorugh goftan (gu)**, to lie

doshman: enemy

dozd: thief

dozdi: theft; **dozdi kardan (kon)**, to steal

dozdidan (dozd): to steal

dowlat: government, state

dowlati: belonging to the state

dowre: around (*prep.*)

doshak: mattress

dud: smoke; **dud kardan (kon)**, to give off smoke

dugh: a drink consisting of yogurt, water and seasoning

dukhtan (duz): to sew

durbin: telescope; binoculars; **durbine akkāsi**, camera (*also just* **durbin**); *adj* long-sighted

dust: friend

dusti: friendship

dush: shower; shoulder

ebtedā: beginning (*see also* **shoru'**)

edāme: continuation; **edāme dādan (deh)**, to continue

edāre: office; **edāre kardan (kon)**, to administer, to manage

eftār: breaking of the fast at sunset in Ramadan

eftekhār: honour; **eftekhār kardan (kon)**, to be proud, to be honoured

eftetāh: inauguration, opening; **eftetāh kardan (kon)**, to inaugurate

eftezāh: disgrace

eghāmat: residence; **ejāzeye eghāmat**, residence permit

eghtesād: economy; economics (*the subject*)

eghtesādi: economical

ehsās: feeling, emotion; **ehsās kardan (kon)**, to feel

ehsāsāti: emotional

ehterām: respect

ehtekār kardan (kon): to hoard; **ehtekār**, hoarding

ehtemāl: possibility, likelihood; **ehtemālesh kam-e**, it's unlikely; **ehtemāl dāre**, it's possible; **be ehtemāle ziād**, in all probability

ehtiāj: need; **ehtiāj dāshtan (dār)**, to need

ehtiāt: care, caution; **bā ehtiāt**, carefully

êivān (*coll.* **êivun**): balcony, verandah

êinak: spectacles

êib: fault; **êib dāshtan (dār)**, to matter; **êib nadāre**, it doesn't matter, never mind

ejāre: rental; **ejāre kardan (kon)**, to rent

ejārenāme: rental agreement, *also sometimes referred to as* **ejarenāmche**

ejāze: permission; **ejāze dādan (deh)**, to give permission; **ejāze gereftan (gir)**, to obtain permission; **ejāze hast?**, may I?

ejbār: obligation; **ejbāri**, obligatory

ejtemā': society; gathering

ejrā kardan (kon): to carry out

ekhtelāf: difference; **ekhtelāf dāshtan (dār)**, to differ

ekhtiār: will

elāhi: divine; **ehlāhi ke** or **elāhi** + *subjunctive* would to God that . . .

e'lān: announcement; **e'lān kardan (kon)**, to announce

e'temād: trust; **e'temād kardan (kon) be**, to trust; **e'temād dāshtan (dār) be**, to trust

e'terāz: protest; **e'terāz kardan (kon)**, to protest

e'tesāb: strike; **e'tesāb kardan (kon)**, to go on strike

emām: spiritual leader

emāmzade: shrine

emkān: possibility; **emkān dāshtan (dār)**, to be possible; **emkān nadāre**, it's impossible

emruz: today

emsāl: this year

emshab: tonight

emtehān: examination, test

emzā: signature

engelestān: England

enghelāb: revolution

enghelābi: revolutionary

enhesār: monopoly

ensān: homo sapiens; one (*the impersonal pronoun*); **folāni ensān-e**, so-and-so is decent

ensāniyyat: decency, humanity

enshā: essay, composition (*literary*)

entekhāb: choice; **entekhāb kardan (kon)**, to choose

entekhābāt: elections

erādat: devotion

erāde: will; **erāde kardan (kon)**, to will; **bā erāde**, strong-willed

ershād: enlightenment; **vezārete ershād**, Ministry of Guidance

ertebāt: connection

esfand: 12th Persian month; incense

eskenās: bank note

eslāh: correction; **eslāh kardan (kon)**, to correct; to shave

eslām: Islam

eslāmi: Islamic

esm: name
espānyā: Spain
espānyoli: Spanish
esrāf: waste
esrār: insistence; **esrār kardan (kon)**, to insist
estaghferollāh: (*lit.* may God forgive me) goodness gracious
ested'ā kardan (kon): to beg (*e.g. a favour*); **ested'ā mikonam**, please (*very polite form*)
este'dād: talent; **bā este'dād**, talented, gifted
este'fā: resignation; **este'fā dādan (deh)**, to resign
estelāh: expression; **be estelāh**, so to speak; as it were
este'mār: imperialism
este'māl: use; **este'māle dokhāniāt mamnu'**, no smoking
estefāde: use, profit; **estefāde kardan (kon)**, to profit; to use (*takes az*)
estefrāgh: vomit; **estefrāgh kardan (kon)**, to be sick
esteghbāl: welcome; **esteghbāl kardan (kon)**, to welcome (*lit. & fig.*)
estekān: small glass, usually for drinking tea
estekhdām kardan (kon): to engage (*in a job*)
esterāhat: rest; **esterāhat kardan (kon)**, to rest
estesmār: exploitation
estesnā: exception; **bedune estesnā**, without exception; **estesnā ghā'el shodan (shav)**, to make exceptions
estesnā'i: exceptional
eshtebāh: mistake; **eshtebāh kardan (kon)**, to make a mistake, to be mistaken
eshtehā: appetite
etā'at: obedience; **etā'at kardan (kon)**, to obey
ettefāgh: occurrence; **ettefāgh oftādan (oftād)**, to happen, to occur
ettehād: unity
ettehādiye: union (*of workers etc.*)
ettelā'āt: information
ezāfe kardan (kon): to add
ezdevāj: marriage; **ezdevāj kardan (kon)**, to get married (*takes bā*)

fa'āl: active; **fa'āliyyat**, activity
fadākāri: self-sacrifice, devotion
faghat: only

faghir (*pl.* **fogharā**): poor

fahm: understanding, intelligence; **fahmidan (fahm)**, to understand

fakk: jaw

falaj: paralysed

falake: roundabout

fanar: spring, coil

fandogh: hazel-nut

farāmush kardan (kon): to forget

farāmushkār: forgetful

farang: word used to refer to Europe in a general sense

farangi: European

farānsavi: French

farānse: France

farār kardan (kon): to run away

farāvān (*coll.* **farāvun**): plentiful

fardā: tomorrow

fargh: difference; parting (*of hair*)

fargh kardan (kon): to change, to alter, to differ

fargh dāshtan (dār): to be different

farhang: culture; dictionary; **vezārate farhang**, Ministry of Education

farmān: order, command

farmān dādan (deh): to give an order

farmānde: commander (*of an army*)

farmudan (farmā): to order; *mostly used to mean* 'to say' *in polite speech* (*but only in 2nd and 3rd persons*)

fasl: season (*of the year*); section (*of a book*)

fāmil: family (*see also* **khānevāde**)

fārsi: Persian (*the language*)

fāsed: corrupt

farzand: offspring, child

fāyde: profit, use; **fāyde nadāre**, it's no use

fehrest: list, index

fekr: thought; **fekr kardan (kon)**, to think

fe'lan: for the time being

felez: metal (*n*); **felezi**, metal (*adj*)

felfel: pepper

fenjān (*coll.* **fenjun**): cup

ferestādan (ferest): to send
fesād: corruption
fesh̲ār: pressure; **fesh̲ār dādan (deh)**, to press, to squeeze
fetr: êide fetr: the festival of the ending of the fasting month of Ramadan on the 1st of Shavval
fil: elephant
firuze: turquoise; also a girl's name
fohs̲h̲: abuse; **fohs̲h̲ dādan (deh)**, to abuse
folān: a certain . . .; **folān kas**, so and so; **folān c̲h̲iz**, such and such
folāni: so and so
forsat: opportunity
forukh̲tan (forus̲h̲): to sell
fowg̲h̲ol'āde: special, extra, very
fowri: urgent
fowt: death
fuzul: meddling

galle: flock (*of sheep*)
galu: throat
galudard: sore throat
gandidan (gand): to go bad, to rot; **gandide**, rotten
gandom: wheat
ganje: cupboard
gard: dust, powder
gardane: mountain pass
gardes̲h̲: outing; turning (*going round*)
garm: warm, hot
gas̲h̲t: patrol
gas̲h̲tan (gard): to turn
gavāhināme: certificate
gaz: a kind of nougat
gāhi: sometimes
gāv: cow
gāz: bite; **gāz gereftan (gir)**, to bite
gāz: gas
gel: mud
gelim: woven rug
gerān (*coll.* gerun): expensive

gerd: round
gere: knot; **gere zadan**, to tie a knot
gereftan (gir): to take, to seize, to take hold of
gerye kardan (kon): to cry
giāh: plant
gij: giddy, dizzy; **sargije**, dizziness
gilās: cherry; drinking glass
gir āmadan (ā): to be available
gir kardan (kon): to get stuck
goftan (gu): to say
gol: flower
golāb: rose-water
golābi: pear
goldān (*coll.* **goldun**): flower-pot, vase
gom kardan (kon): to lose
gom shodan (shav): to be lost, to get lost
gombad: dome
gomrok: customs
gonāh: sin; **gonāh kardan (kon)**, to sin
gonāhkār: sinner (*n*); guilty (*adj*)
gorbe: cat
gorosne: hungry
gowd: deep
gowje: plum
gowjefarangi: tomato
gozāshtan (gozār): to put
gul zadan (zan): to deceive
gunāgun: of different kinds, varied
gur: grave (*n*)
gusāle: calf (*animal*)
gusfand: sheep
gush: ear; **gush kardan (kon)**, to listen
gushe: corner
gushvāre: ear-ring
guyā: it seems, so they say

ghabl: before; **ghabl az**, before
ghablan: beforehand, previously
ghabile: tribe

ghabr: grave (*n*)

ghabrestān: graveyard, cemetery

ghabul kardan (kon): to accept

ghabz: receipt; voucher

ghadam: step, pace

ghadd: stature

ghadim: old, ancient

ghadr: value, worth; size, measure; amount

ghadri: a little

ghahve: coffee

ghalam: pen

ghalat: error, mistake

gham: grief

ghanāt: underground water channels

ghand: loaf sugar

gharār gozāshtan (gozar): to make an arrangement

gharārdad: agreement

gharb: west

gharbi: western

ghargh shodan (shav): to drown

gharib: strange

gharibe: stranger

gharz: loan

ghassāb: butcher

ghassam: oath; ghassam khordan (khor), to take an oath

ghashang: pretty

ghat' kardan (kon): to cut off, to disconnect

ghatār: train

ghatl: killing; in the religious calendar any day commemorating the killing of a religious leader, as opposed to the death, which is **vafāt**

ghavi: strong

ghā'ede: rule

ghāli: carpet

ghānun (*pl.* ghavānin): law

ghārch: mushroom

ghāshogh: spoon

ghāter: mule

ghāyeb: absent

ghāyegh: boat

ghāz: goose

ghêimat: price; **ghêimati**, costly, worth a lot of money

ghêir: other, different; **ghêir az**, other than, except

ghermez: red

ghesmat: portion; lot (*in life*)

ghofl: lock; **ghofl kardan (kon)**, to lock

ghomār: gambling

ghor'ān: the Koran

ghorbāni: sacrificial victim; sacrifice

ghosse: grief

ghotb: pole (*North & South*)

ghowl: promise; **ghowl dadan (deh)**, to promise

ghuri: teapot

ghuti: tin

habs: prison

hadaf: aim, target (*both lit. & fig.*)

hadd: limit

hads: guess; **hads zadan (zan)**, to guess

hafte: week

hagh (*pl.* **hoghugh**): right, due, truth

haghighat: truth

halvā: a kind of sweetmeat

hame: all, everyone

hamkār: colleague

haml: carrying, transport; **haml kardan (kon)**, to transport; **haml o naghl**, transport

hamrāh: together, companion

hamsāye: neighbour

hanuz: still, yet

har: every, each

har gez: never

harāj: auction, sale

harām: forbidden by religious law (*e.g. alcohol, pork etc.*)

harārat: heat

harekat: movement

harf (*pl.* **horuf**): letter

hasir: straw; also a kind of cane blind

hashare (*pl.* **hasharāt**): insect

hasht: eight

hashtād: eighty

hattā: even (*adv*)

havā: air, weather

havāpêımā: aeroplane

havij: carrot

hazine: expenditure; **hazineye zendegi**, the cost of living

hazm: digestion; **hazm kardan (kon)**, to digest

hāfeze: memory

hāl (*pl.* **ahvāl**): health, state, condition

hālā: now

hālat: bearing, manner

hāmele: pregnant

hāzer: ready, present

hedye: present, gift

hefz: preservation

hefz kardan (kon): to learn by heart

hêıf: a pity; what a pity

hêıvan (*coll.* **hêıvun**): animal

hejāb: veil, veiling; **hejābe eslāmi**, Islamic covering for women
    which involves keeping the hair and body totally covered; only
    the face, the hands and the feet (not legs) may be uncovered.

hêı'at: committee; **hêı'at modire**, board of directors

hêıkal: figure, form

hekāyat: a story

hel: cardamom

hendustān: India

hendese: geometry

hendevāne: water melon

hendi: Indian

herfe: craft, trade

hesāb: account, bill; arithmetic

hess: feeling; **hess kardan (kon)**, to feel

hezār: thousand

hezb: political party; **hezbollāh**, the party of God

hich: none, any; **hichvaght**, never; **hichkas**, no one

hizhdah: eighteen

hobubāt: pulses

ho<u>gh</u>ghe: a trick
ho<u>gh</u>u<u>gh</u>: rights; salary, wages; the law (*as a subject*)
hokm: judgement, order, decree
hokumat: government
honar: art
honarpi<u>sh</u>e: actor (*stage or screen*)
how kardan (kon): to ridicule, to heckle
howle: towel
howz: pond
hulu: peach
hu<u>sh</u>: intelligence; **bā hu<u>sh</u>,** intelligent

ijād kardan (kon): to set up, to create, to establish
il: tribe
imān: faith
in (*pl.* **inhā**): this
injā: here
irād: fault; **irād gereftan (gir),** to find fault
irān: Iran
istādan (ist): to stand, to stop
istgāh: stop (*n*) (*for buses, trains, taxis etc.*)
ist: stop!
i<u>sh</u>ān: they
itāliā: Italy
itāliā'i: Italian

ja'be: box
jabr: algebra
jadid: new
jahān: world
jahāngard: tourist
jahat: direction; **be in jahat,** for this reason
jahāz: dowry
jam': addition; gathering, group
jang: war
jangal: forest
jaryān: flow, circulation, happening; **jaryān <u>ch</u>iye?,** what goes
   on?, what's it all about?
jarime: fine

jarrāh: surgeon

jarresaghil: crane (*mechanical*)

jashn: celebration; **jashn gereftan (gir)**, to celebrate

javāb: answer, reply; **javāb dadan (deh)**, to answer

javān: young

javāz: permit

jazire (*pl.* **jazāyer**): island

jā: place

jādde: road, highway

jāleb: interesting; **jālebe tavajjoh**, worth noting

jāme'e: society; community

jān: soul, life

jāru: broom

jāsus: spy

jebhe: war front, battle front

jeddi: serious, earnest

jeld: volume; binding of a book

jelo: front (*n*); **jelo(ye)**, in front of

jelogiri kardan (kon): to prevent

jens: kind, sort, species

jim shodan (shav): to slip away (*fig.*), *i.e. to leave without being
    noticed*

jib: pocket

jire: ration

jirebandi: rationing

jobrān kardan (kon): to make up for

jodā: separate; **jodā kardan (kon)**, to separate; **jodā shodan (shav)**,
    to be separated

joft: pair (*n*)

jom'e: Friday

jomle: sentence

jomhuri: republic; **jomhuriye eslāmi**, Islamic Republic

jonub: South

jorm: crime

jostan (ju): to seek; (*coll.*) to find; **jostish?**, did you find it?

jow: barley

joz: except

jub: ditch; water channel by the side of the street

juje: chicken

jur: kind, sort
jurāb: socks, stockings
jush: boil (*n*)
jushidan (jush): to boil

kabāb: usu. meat cooked over charcoal, kebab, but anything
   cooked over charcoal is **kabāb kardé**
kafsh: shoe
kaj: crooked
kalāntari: police station
kamar: waist
kamarband: belt
kandan (kan): to dig; to take off (*clothes*); to remove
kardan (kon): to do
kare: butter
kas (*coll.* **kes**): person
kasif: dirty
kashk: dried buttermilk
kāj: fir tree
kāghaz: paper
kāh: chaff; **mesle pare kāh**, as light as a feather
kār: work; **kār kardan (kon)**, to work
kārd: knife
kāshtan (kār): to plant
ke: that
kebrit: matches
kelid (*coll.* **kilid**): key
kerāye: hire; fare (*bus, taxi etc.*); rental (*house etc.*)
keshidan (kesh): to draw (*pictures*); to pull; to suffer (*coll.*)
keshvar: country
ketāb: book
ketri: kettle
ki: who
kif: bag
kise: sack; a stiff washglove
kohne: (*n*) rag; (*adj*) old (*things*)
kolā: hat
kollan: overall; in general
koloft: thick

kond: blunt (*not sharp*); slow
koshtan (kosh): to kill
kuche: street
kuchik: small
kuh: mountain
kushidan (kush): to try
kutā: short

khabar (*pl.* akhbār): news
khalās: free
khalabān: pilot
khalij: gulf (*geog.*)
khamir: paste; dough
kham shodan (shav): to bend (*intrans.*)
kham kardan (kon): to bend (*trans.*)
khande: laughter
khandidan (khand): to laugh
khar: ass, donkey
kharāb: out of order, broken
kharāsh: scratch (*n*)
khargush: rabbit, hare
kharidan (khar): to buy
kharj: expenditure, expense; **kharj kardan (kon)**, to spend
khardal: mustard
khaste: tired; **khaste shodan (shav)** (*intrans.*) to get tired; **khaste kardan (kon)** (*trans.*), to make tired
khatar: danger
khatarnāk: dangerous
khatt: line; writing
khatm: mourning ceremony
khayyāt: tailor, dressmaker
khārāndan (khārān): to scratch
khāresh: itching
khārbār: foodstuffs
khārbār forushi: grocer's
khāridan (khār): to itch
khāstan (khāh): to want
khastegāri: asking in marriage
khāb: sleep
khābidan (khāb): to sleep

khāhar: sister

khāk: dust; earth; territory

khākestar: ashes

khāle: maternal aunt

khāles: pure (*things*)

khāli: empty

khām: raw

khāmush: silent; out (*fire, light*)

khāmush kardan (kon): to put out (*a fire, a light*); to turn off (*an engine, the radio etc.*)

khāme: cream

khāne: house

khānum: lady

khārej: outside; abroad

khāreji: foreigner; foreign

khāstan (khāh): to want

khāter: memory; sake; **bekhātere . . .**, for the sake of; **khāteram nist/be khāter nadaram**, I don't remember

khāter jam': assured, confident; **khāteram jam' bud**, my mind was at ease; **khāteret jam' bāshe**, set your mind at rest, rest assured

khedmat: service

khedmatgār: servant

khejālat: shame, embarrassment; **khejālat keshidan (kesh)**, to be ashamed or embarrassed

khesārat: damage

khêır: no

khêır: goodness

khêıriyye: charity

khiābān (*coll.* **khiābun**): road, street

khiāl: thought; **khiāl kardan (kon)**, to think

khiār: cucumber

khis: wet

khod: self

khodā: God

khodnevis: fountain pen

khorāk: food

khordan (khor): to eat

khoresht: Persian stew to accompany rice

khormā: date
khorshid: sun
khoruj: exit
khorus: cock
khosh: happy; **khosh gozashtan (gozar)**, to have a good time
khoshk: dry
khoshgel: pretty
khosusi: private
khub: good
khuk: pig
khun: blood; **khun āmadan (ā)** (*intrans.*), to bleed

labe: edge
labriz: overflowing
labu: cooked beetroot
lagad: kick; **lagad zadan (zan)**, to kick; **lagad kardan (kon)**, to
   kick *or* step on
lahn: tone (*of voice*)
lahāz:: **az lahāze**, from the point of view of, in terms of
lahestān: Poland
lahje: accent
lajbāz: obstinate
lak: spot, stain; **lak kardan (kon)**, to stain
lang: lame
la'nat: curse
lappe: yellow split peas
larzidan (larz): to shiver
lashkar: army, division
lā: fold
lāye: in, between
lābod: probably
lāghar: thin
lāhāf: quilt
lāl: dumb
lāle: tulip
lāyehe: bill (*parliamentary*)
lāzem: necessary; **lāzem dashtan (dār)**, to need
lebās: clothes
lezzat: pleasure; **lezzat bordan (bar)**, to enjoy

limu: lemon; **limu torsh**, sour lemon, lime; **limu shirin** sweet
lemon
lisidan (lis): to lick
livān: glass (*for drinking*)
liz: slippery
lokht: naked
loghat: word
lubiā: bean, *usually means white haricot beans*; **lubiā sabz**, French
beans; **lubiā ghermez**, red kidney beans; **lubiā chiti**, pinto
beans
lule: pipe (*for water etc.*); **lule kardan (kon)** (*trans.*) to make into
a roll
lulekesh: plumber
lus: spoilt (*child etc.*)

mabādā: lest; **ruze mabādā**, a rainy day
ma'dan: mine (*both lit. and fig.*)
madrese (*pl.* **madāres** & *coll.* **madresehā**): school
magas: fly (*n*)
maghreb: west
maghsud: object
mahal: place
mahāl: impossible
mahsul: harvest
mahtāb: moonlight
mahzar: notary public's office
majbur: obliged, forced (to do sth.)
majalle: magazine
majles: assembly; parliament; **majlese showrāye eslāmi**, Islamic
Consultative Assembly: the Iranian parliament
makhsus: special
malāfe: sheet (*on a bed*)
mamnu': forbidden, prohibited
mamnun: thankful, grateful
ma'mur: official *n*
man: I, me
ma'ni: meaning
manzel: house
mard: man

mardom: people

mariz: ill

maraz: illness; *also used in slang as a term of abuse, something on the lines of* 'shut up' *only worse*

marsum: customary

martabe: time; **yek martabe**, once; **chand martabe**, several times

martub: moist, damp

markaz: centre

marz: frontier

mas'ale: question (*in the sense of a problem*)

masjed: mosque

mashmul: due for conscription

mashregh: east

mashrub: drink (*usually refers to alcoholic drink*)

ma'zerat: apology; **ma'zerat khāstan (khāh)**, to apologise

mazhab: religion

mazze: taste

mā: we

mādar: mother; **mādar zan**, mother-in-law (*wife's mother*); **mādar showhar**, mother-in-law (*husband's mother*)

māch: kiss

māshāllā: what God wills; *an expression used as a kind of verbal touching wood*

māsse: sand

māst: yoghurt

māh: moon; **mesle māh**, beautiful, very nice; **māh-e**, (*said of people or things*) it/he/she is extremely nice

māhi: fish

māhiāne: monthly (*coll.* **māhyune**)

māl: wealth, riches, possessions; **māle**, belonging to

mālek: owner

māliāt: tax; **māliāt bar darāmad**, income tax

māli: financial

mālidan (māl): to rub

māndan (mān): to stay

mār: snake

māshin: car; machine

māye': liquid

mehmān (*coll.* **mehmun**): guest

mehrabān: loving
melli: national
mesle: like, similar
mêidān: square
mêil: preference
mesr: Egypt
mesri: Egyptian
mikh: nail
mive: fruit
miz: table
mo'allem: teacher
mo'āven: deputy, assistant
modir: director
moddat: period of time
mofid: useful
moghābel(e): opposite
mohandes: engineer
mohassel: student
mohkam: firm
mohr: seal
mojāz: permitted
mokhtasar: brief
momken: possible
monshi: secretary
morabbā: jam
morabba': squared
mordād: 5th Persian month
mordan (mir): to die
morgh: hen; chicken
mosāfer: traveller
mosāferat: journey; **mosāferat kardan** to travel
mosbat: positive, affirmative
mostarā: lavatory
moshkel: difficult
mosht: fist, handful
moshtari: customer
mota'assef: sorry, regretful
moteshakker: thankful
motābeghe: according to

mottahed: united
movāfeghat: agreement
mowj: wave
mowz: banana
mozakhraf: nonsense, rubbish
mozd: wage
mu: hair
mush: mouse
mushak: rocket

nafar: person
naft: petroleum; kerosene
naghghāsh: painter
naghshe: map, plan
najjār: carpenter
nakhl: palm tree
nam: damp (*n*); **namnāk**, damp (*adj*)
namak: salt
narm: soft
nazar: thought, opinion; **benazare man**, to my mind
nāgahān: suddenly
nāhār: lunch
nām: name
nāme: letter
nān (*coll.* **nun**): bread
nāshtāi: breakfast
negāh: look; **negāh kardan (kon)**, to look
nesf: half
neshastan (neshin): to sit
neshān dādan (deh): to show
neshāni: address
neveshtan (nevis): to write
nezāmi: military
nim: half
niru: strength, power; **vezārate niru**, Ministry of Energy
niz: also
noghre: silver
noghte: dot, full stop
nowkar: manservant

nomre: number, mark (*in examination*)
now: new

ofogh: horizon
oftādan (oft): to fall
ojāgh: stove
olāgh: donkey
ommat: congregation
omid: hope
omidvār: hopeful
ons: attachment; **ons gereftan (gir) (be)**, to become attached (to)
ordak: duck
ordibehesht: 2nd Persian month
orupā: Europe
orupāi: European
ostād: professor; expert
ostān: province
ostokhān: bone
otāgh: room
owlād: offspring, children
ozr: excuse; **ozr khāstan (khāh)**, to ask forgiveness, to make excuses
ozv (*pl.* **a'zā**): member

pahlu: side
pambe: cotton wool
panir: cheese
panjere: window
parcham: flag
pardākhtan (pardāz): to pay
parde: curtain
pariruz: the day before yesterday
pasandidan (pasand): to approve of, to like
patu: blanket
pazirāi: entertainment (*hospitality*); reception
pā: foot
pāin: down; **pāin(e)**, at the bottom of
pāiz: autumn
pāk: clean

pākat: envelope; packet; paper bag
pālto: overcoat
pārche: material
pāre: torn
pārsāl: last year
pārti: influence
pāru: oar; a flat wide shovel used for clearing snow
pāsdār (*pl.* **pāsdārān**): guard
pedar: father
pelle: step, stair
pêida: apparent, visible; **pêida kardan (kon)**, to find
pesar: boy, son
peste: pistachio nut
pich: screw
pichāndan (pichān): to turn (*trans.*)
pichidan (pich): to turn (*intrans.*); to wrap up
pir: old
pishraft: progress; **pishraft kardan (kon)**, to make progress
piāderow: pavement
piāz: onion
pokhtan (paz): to cook
pol: bridge
polo: pillau rice
porsidan (pors): to ask, to enquire
post: post
posht: back; **poshte**, behind
pul: money
pust: skin
pustin: a kind of sheepskin jacket
pushidan (push): to wear
putin: boots

ra'd: thunder
rad shodan (shav): to pass by; to fail (*an exam*)
rafigh: friend, chum
raftan (rav): to go
raftār: behaviour
raghs: dance
raghsidan (raghs): to dance

ra'is (*pl.* **ro'asā**): boss, head, chief
rakhtekhāb: bedding, bedclothes
rang: colour, paint; **rang kardan (kon)**, to dye, to paint
rasmi: official
rāh: road, way
rāhat: comfortable
rāje'be: concerning, about
rāndan (rān): to drive
rast: right, true, straight
residan (res): to arrive
rikhtan (riz): to pour; to spill
roshve: bribe
rotubat: damp
rowghan: fat; oil
rowshan: light; **rowshan kardan (kon)**, to light, to turn on, to switch on
ru: face; **ruye**, on top of; **por ru**, cheeky
rude: intestine
rudkhāne: river
ruz: day
ruze: fast; **ruze gereftan (gir)**, to fast. Fasting involves having nothing to eat or drink between the hours of sunrise and sunset in the month of Ramadan.
ruzmarre: daily (*in the sense of every-day*)
ruznāme: newspaper

sabr: patience; **sabr kardan (kon)**, to wait
sabz: green
sabzi: (*lit.* greenery) *usually refers to the many varieties of green herbs such as parsley, dill, coriander etc. used in preparing Persian dishes. The plural* **sabzijāt** *is used in restaurants etc. to refer to vegetables.*
sadd: dam
safar: journey; **safar kardan** to travel
saf: queue; **saf bastan (band)**, to queue
safir (*pl.* **sofarā**): ambassador
safhe: sheet (*of paper, metal etc*); page (*of a book*)
sag: dog (*considered unclean by Moslems*)
sahih: correct

sahm: share, portion

sahām: (*pl.* of **sahm**) shares (*in a company, on the stock exchange etc.*)

sakht: difficult, hard; **in kār sakht-e**, this job is difficult; **folāni sakht mashghul-e**, so-and-so is hard at work/very busy

salmāni (*coll.* **salmuni**): hairdresser; barber

san'at (*pl.* **sanāye'**): industry; **sanāye'e sangin**, heavy industry

sandali: chair

sandogh: large box, chest; cash register, till; **gāv sandogh**, safe

sang: stone

sangin: heavy

sanjāgh: pin; hair pin

sar: head (*anatomical*); top; **sare kuh**, at the top of the hill; **sare rāh(e)**, on the way (to); **sare khiabun, sare meîdun, sare kuche**, *mean* at the top of, at, at the end of, *depending on the vantage point of the speaker and are very common expressions*

sarbāz: soldier (*lit. one who loses his head*)

sard: cold (*adj*)

sarhadd: frontier

sarmā: cold (*n*); **sarmā khordan (khor)**, to catch cold; **sarmā khordegi**, the common cold; **sarmā khordam/khordé-am**, I've got a cold

sarv: Cypress (tree)

savād: literacy; **bāsavād**, literate; **bisavād**, illiterate; **bisavādi**, illiteracy

savāri: riding

sa'y kardan (kon): to try; **kheîli sa'y kard**, he tried hard

sā'at: hour; watch; clock; the time

sābegh: former

sāde: plain (*adj*)

sāder kardan (kon): to export

sāderāt: exports

sāheb: owner; **sāhebkhune** (*coll.* **sābkhune**), landlord/lady

sakht: difficult

sakhtan (saz): to build, to make

sakhtemān: building; construction

sāl: year

sālgard: anniversary

sāye: shadow; shade

sedā: sound; noise; voice; **sedā kardan (kon)**, to call, to make a noise; **sedā zadan (zan)**, to call

sefārat: embassy

sefāresh: order, recommendation; **sefāresh dadan (deh)**, to place an order; **sefāresh kardan (kon)**, to make a recommendation (*usu. to recommend sth. or someone to someone else*)

sefid: white

seft: hard, tough (*usu. refers to texture*)

sêil: flood

senn: age

sepāh: *literally means* an army *or* army division, *but nowadays used to refer to the* **sepāhe pāsdārān**, *or just* **sepāh**, the force of revolutionary guards

setāre: star; **setāreye sinemā**, film star

siāh: black

sib: apple

sibzamini: potato (*originally* **sibe zamini**)

sigār: cigarette

sim: wire

sine: breast, chest

sini: tray

so'āl: question; **so'āl kardan (kon)**, to ask a question

sob: morning

sombol: hyacinth

shabe shambe: Friday night (*lit.* Saturday eve)

shenidan (shenav): to hear

sherkat: company; participation

sheved (*coll.* **shivid**): dill

shir: milk; lion

shirin: sweet; also a girl's name

shirini: sweetness; sweetmeats

shishe: glass, bottle

sho'be: branch (*of a bank, business etc.*)

shoghl (*pl.* **mashāghel**): occupation, profession

shol: loose

sho'le: flame

shomāre: number

shoru': beginning; **shoru' kardan (kon)**, to begin (*trans.*); **shoru' shodan (shav)**, to begin (*intrans.*)

shotor: camel
showhar: husband
shukhi: joke
shur: salt (*adj*)

ta'ajjob: surprise
tab: fever
tabi'at: nature
tabi'i: natural
tafrih: amusement, fun (*but not in the sense of humour*)
taghriban: almost, nearly
taghsir: fault; **taghsir dashtan (dar)**, to be at fault; **taghsire man nist**, it's not my fault
taghvim: diary, calendar
taghyir: change; **taghyir kardan (kon)**, to change
tahvil: hand-over; **tahvil dadan (deh)**, to hand over, to deliver
tajrobe: experience
takān (*coll.* **takun**): shake; **takun dādan (deh)**, to shake (*trans.*); **takun khordan (khor)**, to shake (*intrans.*)
taklif: duty, task; **taklife man o rowshan kon**, make up your mind what you want me to do; **bela taklif budan**, to be in a state of not knowing what one is supposed to do
talab: that which is owing to you; **ye toman talabe man**, you owe me one toman; **azesh talab dāram**, he owes me
talkh: bitter
tamām (*coll.* **tamum**): whole, complete; **tamām kardan (kon)**, to finish (*trans.*); **tamām shodan (shav)**, to finish (*intrans.*)
tamāshā: watching; sightseeing
tambāku: tobacco
tambal: lazy
tambr: stamp (*postage and for various kinds of duty*)
tan: body (*anatomical*)
tanāb: rope
tane: trunk; **taneye derakht**, tree trunk; **bālā tane**, upper part of the body; bodice
tang: narrow; tight
tar: wet
taraf: side, direction; **be tarafe**, towards
tarafdār: supporter
tarak: crack; **tarakidan (tarak)**, to burst

tarāshidan (tarāsh): to shave
tare: an onion-tasting herb like a very fine leek
tare farangi: leek
tarkhun: tarragon
tars: fear
tarsidan (tars): to be afraid
taryāk: opium
tarz: method
tasavvor: imagination, thought
tasdigh: certificate; **tasdighe rānandegi**, driving licence
tasfiye: refining (*of oil etc.*); purification (*of water*)
taslim: surrender; **khod rā taslim kardan (kon)**, *or* **taslim shodan (shav)**, to surrender
tasmim: decision; **tasmim gereftan (gir)**, to decide
tasvir: drawing, picture
tashrifāt: ceremonial, protocol
ta'til (*pl.* **ta'tilāt**): holiday; (*adj*) closed (*of shops etc.*)
tavallod: birth; **jashne tavallod**, birthday party
tavānā: able
tavānestan (tavān): to be able
tayyāre: aeroplane
tā: until; fold; **tā kardan (kon)**, to fold
tāb: swing
tābestān: summer
tājer: merchant
tāksi: taxi
tārikh: history, date
tāze: fresh
tejārat: trade, commerce
teshne: thirsty
teshnegi: thirst
tir: shot, bullet; **tir khordan (khor)**, to be shot
tofang: gun
tokhm: seed, egg; **tokhme morgh**, egg; **tokhme**, cured salted melon seeds
tolombe: pump
tond: fast, quick, rapid; hot (*of flavours*)
towr: way, means: **intowr**, thus; **untowr**, like that; **b: towrike**, in such a way that; **har towr shodé**, whatever happens (*however much it takes*)

tul: length; **tul dādan (deh)**, to take a long time; **tul keshidan (kesh)**, to take a long time; **chera inghadr tul dādi**, why did you take so long; **(kāram) tul keshid**, (my work *or* it) took me a long time

tulāni: lengthy

tup: ball (*for games*); cannon

utu: iron (*for clothes*); **utu kardan (kon)**, to iron

va: and

vaght (*pl.* **owghāt**) time; **ba'zi vaghthā**, sometimes; **ba'zi owghāt**, sometimes

vakil: lawyer; deputy; **vakile majles**, member of parliament; legal representative

varagh: playing cards; sheet (*of paper*), e.g. **chand varagh kāghaze sefid lāzem dāram**, I need a few/several sheets of white paper; **varagh zadan (zan)**, to turn the page (*of a book etc.*)

varaghe: a piece of paper

varzesh: sport, exercise

varzeshkār: sportsman

vasat: middle

vasile: means, equipment

vatan: native country

vazife: duty; **nezam vazife**, military service

vazir: minister; **nakhost vazir**, prime minister

vā: (*excl.*) oh!, really?

vāghe'i: true, actual

vāhed: unit

vām: loan

vān: bathtub

vāred shodan (shav): to enter

vāredāt: imports

vel kardan (kon): to let go of

vojud: existence; **vojud dāshtan (dār)**, to exist

yaghin: certainty; *much used in speech to mean* 'most probably', 'almost certainly'

yakh: ice; **yakh zadé**, frozen (*of things*)

yakhchāl: refrigerator

yavāsh: slowly; quietly

yād: memory
yād gereftan (gir): to learn
yāddāsht: note
yās: jasmine, lilac

zabān: tongue; language
zahmat: trouble; **zahmat keshidan (kesh)**, to take pains, to work hard
zakhm: wound
zamān: time
zambur: bee
zambil: basket
zan: woman, wife
zang: bell; rust; **zang zadan (zan)**, to ring; to rust
zanjir: chain
zarb: multiplication
zarbe: blow (*n*)
zard: yellow
zardālu: apricot
zarf (*pl.* **zoruf**, *also* **zarfhā**): dish
zarfiyyat: capacity
zarfshu'i: dishwasher
zā'idan (zā): to give birth
zānu: knee; **zānu zadan (zan)**, to kneel
zebr: rough
zedde: against
zemestān: winter
zendān: prison
zende: alive
zendegi: life, living
ziād: a lot, much
ziārat: pilgrimage
zibā: beautiful; girl's name
zire: under
zoghāl: charcoal
zohr: noon, midday
zud: early; quick
zur: force, strength; **be zur**, by force

zhele: jelly